the OLD HANGTOWN ROAD

CAROL D. MACAULAY

The Old Hangtown Road
Copyright © 2026 by Carol D. Macaulay

Library of Congress Control Number: 2026904609

ISBN (print): 979-8-9948165-0-9
ISBN (ebook): 979-8-9948165-1-6

Interior design by Damonza
Cover design by Damonza

Published by Carol D. Macaulay
The Forks Plantation, Maine
Printed in the United States of America

This book is dedicated to the early settlers of Hangtown
and to today's voyagers who seek the history and
amusements along the old Hangtown Road.

Contents

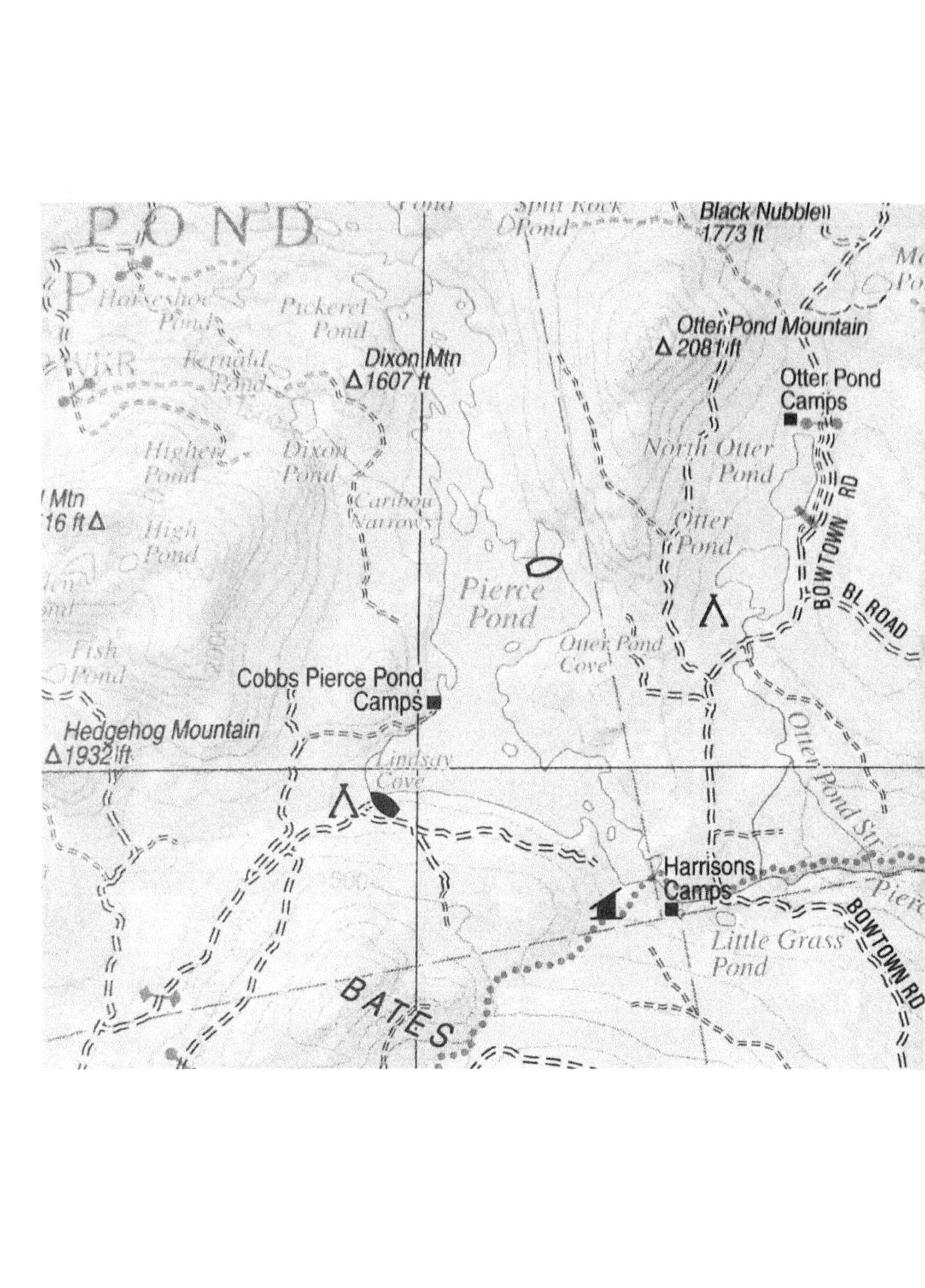

P O N D
P
Horseshoe Pond
Pickerel Pond
VXR
Fernald Pond
Dixon Mtn
△1607 ft
Split Rock Pond
Black Nubble
1,773 ft
Mo Po
Otter Pond Mountain
△ 2081 ft
Otter Pond Camps
Higher Pond
Dixon Pond
North Otter Pond
Mtn
16 ft △
High Pond
Caribou Narrows
Otter Pond
BOWTOWN RD
BL ROAD
Pierce Pond
Fish Pond
Otter Pond Cove
Cobbs Pierce Pond Camps
Lindsay Cove
Otter Pond Str
Hedgehog Mountain
△1932 ft
Harrisons Camps
Little Grass Pond
BOWTOWN RD
Pierc
Pierce
BATES

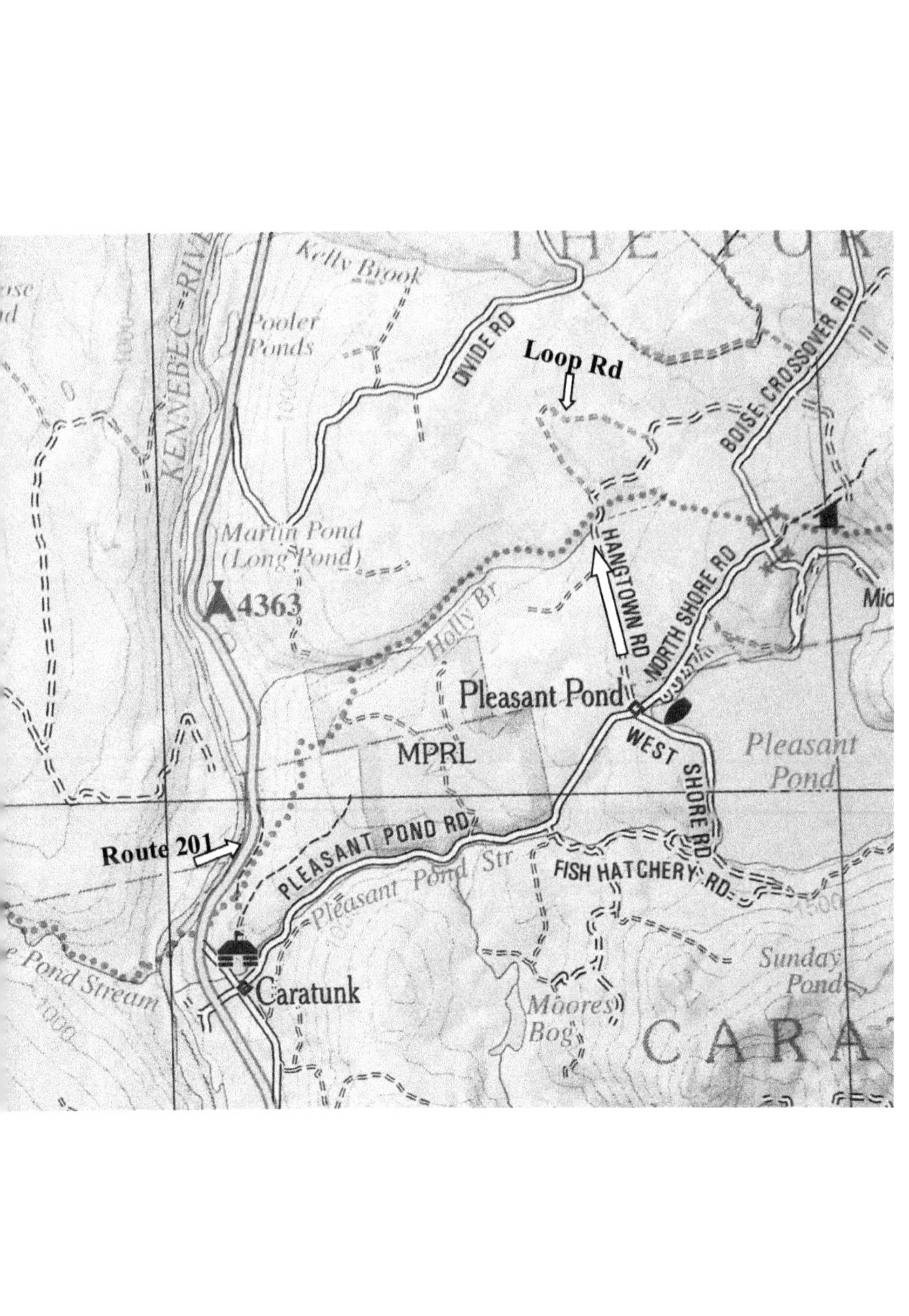

THE FOR
Kelly Brook
Pooler Ponds
KENNEBEC RIVER
DIVIDE RD
Loop Rd
BOISE CROSSOVER RD
Martin Pond
(Long Pond)
4363
Holly Br
HANGTOWN RD
Mid
Pleasant Pond
NORTH SHORE RD
MPRL
WEST SHORE RD
Pleasant Pond
Route 201
PLEASANT POND RD
Pleasant Pond Str
FISH HATCHERY RD
Pond Stream
Caratunk
Moores Bog
Sunday Pond
CARA

Preface

My purpose is not just to recount the history of Hangtown, but to invite you, the reader, to step into Hangtown's world—to walk its roads with an appreciation for the lives that once lived there. By sharing the settlers' stories—their challenges, joys, and triumphs—I hope to preserve their legacy. It was once a thriving, energetic yet very small community—a past that evokes nostalgia, emotion, beauty and hope.

As I uncovered the story behind Hangtown Road's name, I unearthed the rich history of Hangtown—the settlers, their livelihoods, their fortitude—and I felt the responsibility to pass this knowledge on to others who are drawn to its story.

This book is more than a collection of stories. It is a testament to the lives and spirit of Hangtown's people. As you turn these pages, I hope that you'll feel the echoes of their footsteps, their resilience, their determination, and yet sometimes resignation, and you'll come to appreciate the enduring connection between the past and the present.

My hope is that this book, with its stories woven from true facts, folklore, and imaginative twists, helps history survive.

Acknowledgements

My sincere thanks to Julie Richards of the Old Canada Road Historical Society. Her passion for preserving and sharing the local history brought authenticity to my book.

I am also grateful to: Allen Later of Old Canada Historical Society for his help in identifying old maps and roads; William Henry Sizeland for generously contributing pictures of his ancestors and the old farm in Hangtown; Tom Reed, Fred Curran, and many others who offered their knowledge, stories, and experiences regarding Hangtown; and to the personnel at The Forks Plantation Town Office for allowing me to research old town records at leisure.

Special thanks to Marlene Lawson, who offered valuable edits and thoughtful guidance.

I am especially grateful to Larry Fuller, who stood by me through every stage of writing this book and patiently forgave the countless hours I spent buried in research, surrounded by piles of papers, notebooks, and writing paraphernalia that took over our very small home.

Introduction

As the years have passed, Hangtown has transformed from a community of farmers and loggers—its community dispersed, its road quiet, and its structures reclaimed by nature. Yet its story endures, whispered through the trees and carried by the wind. By sharing these stories, I hope to honor not just the settlers, but the spirit of places like Hangtown that leave an indelible mark on the ears of those who take time to listen.

I will lead you through the history of the area—into the lives of the early settlers, the turning over of property, and the stories, folklore, spirits and mysteries that make Hangtown unique. Old lives and new lives—old purpose and new!

"History is a fiction created by those who survive."

–Linda Tatelbaum,
Carrying Water–A Way of Life.

Chapter 1

A QUICK HISTORY
OF THE AREA

Previously Maine was part of Massachusetts after the English drove the Norridgewock, a branch of the Abenaki Indians, out of the territory.

In 1791, the Upper Kennebec, called the Million Acres, was surveyed by Samuel Western and Samuel Titcomb for the Massachusetts Commission on Eastern Lands. It was sold to Henry Jackson and Royal Flint, who were agents for Gen. Henry Knox and Col. William Duer. Included in the purchase was a sales agreement which stated that by 1803, twenty-five hundred settlers had to be established on the land.

However, by 1792 Col. Duer found himself in financial difficulties and Gen. Knox convinced William Bingham, a wealthy Philadelphian businessman, to buy Duer's interest. On December 31, 1792 a purchase agreement was made and by the end of January, 1793 the contract was done in Bingham's name only. Attached to the contract was what is called "settling duties". The purchaser needed to have a number of persons settled in five years and increase that number within twelve years on this tract of land. Bingham was busy with another tract of land he had purchased and did not get around to establishing a plan for the settling of the Kennebec Tract. It was better known as the Kennebec Millions or Bingham's Million Acres. Some settlers were slowly migrating from the southern areas and homesteading on his land. These settlers were eager to buy their lots but Bingham was slow at responding. To encourage the settlements, roads were the responsibility of the Tract owners. Massachusetts legislature wanted a road opened from the northern most townships to Quebec. Bingham only had to build the road through his tract of land.

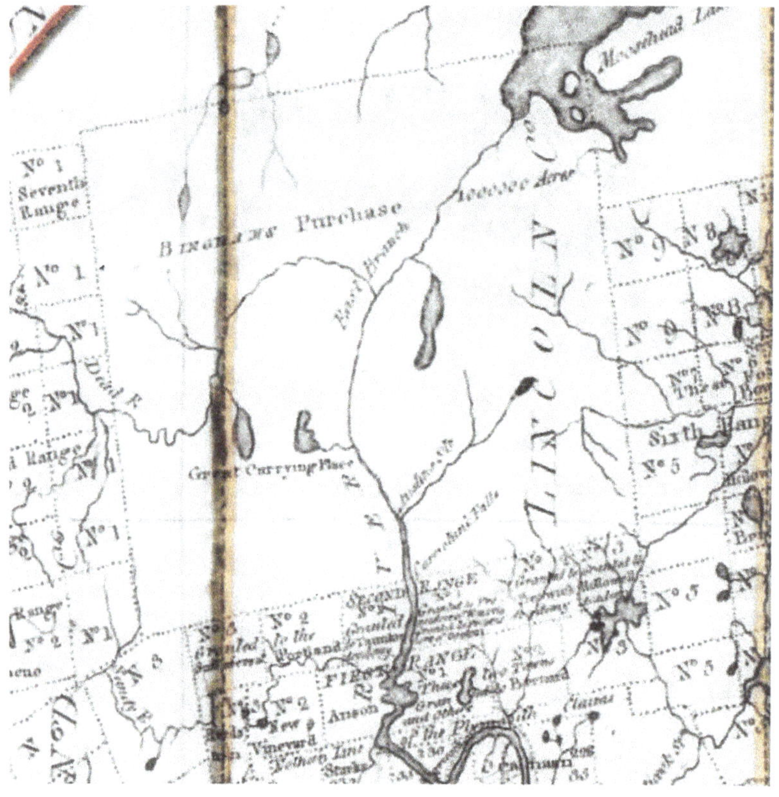

Image 1. Bingham's Purchase

In 1804, William Bingham died suddenly and the trustees were left with administering his huge estate including the "Kennebec Million".

This was a very slow process without much attention from the trustees. Bingham's Kennebec Millions trustees had to now take on the responsibility to create a design and get the road built north through this Bingham tract. It was also necessary for them to come up with a price per acre so the settlers could buy their homesteads they had been promised.

As previously stated, many settlers had traveled to Bingham's Acres homesteading. They built homes and businesses without owning the land. They were still waiting for purchase agreements from the Trustees. Some homesteaders moved on, not selling the land but their improvements such as houses, inns, businesses, and farms.

Finally, in 1810, Massachusetts legislature resolved to build a road from the Kennebec River to the River Chaudiere, Canada right through the Bingham's Kennebec Million. The "Old Canada Road" road was originally surveyed for the Massachusetts's Legislature by John Neal and Thomas McKechnie and was finally approved 1810-11. The Bingham trustees, responsible for the road going through the Bingham Kennebec Million, were to survey and submit an acceptable plan for the road. However, the road was delayed due to the War of 1812, and Bingham's acceptable plan was never drawn up.

The road project resumed in 1817. James Irish was commissioned to do a new survey for the road, from Bingham's Million Acres north border to the Canada border. It took Irish and crew from August 9, 1817 to September 19, 1817 to do this. The plan was submitted on Jan 8, 1818.

Bingham's trustee's (proprietors) were given a deadline and ultimatum to formulate an acceptable plan to build their portion of the road or the Courts would take over and build a road of their own design through Bingham's territory.

In 1818, the Somerset County Court having no faith in the proprietors' responding with an acceptable road design, ordered the construction of the road to begin. This road would follow an old Indian trail up the west side of the Kennebec River.

The early settlers, encouraged to settle in this region, found the soil fertile but rocky. They could grow an abundance of corn and grain but no way to convert it into food. The road was barely better now and the nearest grist mill was in Norridgewock. This was a two-day trip by canoe, with two days needed for the return journey back with their flour.

In 1824, a petition was made and accepted to build a more practical road on the east side of the Kennebec, including a bridge across the Kennebec at the forks of the river. Many of The Forks settlers eager to own their homesteads, helped build the road and bridge, with their wages applied to what they owed for their lots. The sales took place between 1807 and 1830. Some were able to pay for them entirely. The road was completed around 1859.

The Forks is where the Dead River (upper center) and the Kennebec (right) come together before the bridge as one goes north. The area south of the bridge is called The Forks Village (The Forks Plantation). North of the bridge is the town of The West Forks.

CHAPTER 2

BEFORE THE RIVER ROAD → OLD CANADA ROAD → RT 201

IMMIGRANTS, FROM OR by way of Canada, were among the early settlers searching for a better life in a new land. Only an Indian and trapper's trail existed from Quebec, to the district of Maine (Massachusetts). It was much like a ghostly footpath, meandering through the rough territory of Canada and the rugged forests of Maine. Immigrants followed that same path that Benedict Arnold took on his march to Quebec. Following Arnold's trail south would take them from Quebec to La Beauce, Sartigan, Lac Megantic, and into Maine. It continued to West, Middle, and East Carry Ponds through The Dead River Territory, over The Great Carrying Place between the Dead River and The Kennebec River; and finally ended at Carrying Place Stream on Wyman Lake, Caratunk.

How better to explain the plights of determined immigrants

than to reprint an article I found in the March 26, 1903 issue of The Somerset Reporter. This venture took place in 1815 with the article having been originally published in 1873.

The death of Nancy McCollar Sands brings to the memory of the older residents of Skowhegan and other (surrounding towns in Piscataquis County) the story published in the REPORTER some thirty years ago (which would have been 1873) of the hardships and sufferings her father and mother experienced in getting to this country. It was in the year 1815 that Patrick McCollar and his wife left Derry, Ireland, in March with their children, Barnard, aged 18 months and Nancy, three weeks old. After six weeks and three days' voyage they landed at Quebec, going from there to St. George, where they remained until the following October, when they started for Madison, Maine, through the woods by a spotted line. Mrs. McCollar was the second white woman to start on foot and the first one to get through, as the first woman, the unfortunate Mrs. Phobers, died on the road with cold and hunger.

They started with six days' provisions and were twelve days on the road, her pack weighing 20 pounds with her six months' old baby, he with 60 pounds pack and the two-year old boy. After seven days' tramp, camping on the ground nights and suffering with the cold, foot sore and weary, they got to The Forks of the Kennebec River, there being no bridge they were forced to wade the river. He took her pack and the baby Nancy got her across safely, in the meentime (meantime) he had to tie the little boy, Barney, to a tree until he could come back for him. The child cried with fright when he saw them leave him. He was obliged to tie him or he would run into the river.

After this when they got down four or five miles, they came to what is called now the John Stuart place, a small clearing with a hut on it and a fire smouldering (smoldering). They found a few potatoes someone had planted, they dug and roasted some in the fire, thanking God for food and shelter. They rested until the next day, then, with fresh courage, they once more started on their journey.

When they arrived at what is now the pretty town of Bingham it was nothing but a chopping with a few log houses. If there were any frame ones they did not notice them, and the town of Solon was merely a chopping also.

Their journey ended at the place called the Captain Ben Thomson farm just above the Patterson Bridge, later called the Albert Manerly farm. Patrick McCollar settled there and raised a family of ten boys and two girls. The oldest boy, Barney, whom he brought through with him, enlisted and died in the Mexican war from wounds received there. To the war of '61-'64, he gave five sons and two grandsons, and they were all at one time in active service. All that are left of his sons are John of St. George, Canada, Edward of Solon, Me., and Peter F., of Minnesota.

More than 500,000 people immigrated to the manufacturing mills in Maine, Massachusetts and Rhode Island between 1813 and 1859.

Of course, we know most of the path that travelers initially followed was later better defined through hard labor, eventually becoming the road to Canada on the west side of the Kennebec River. Yet it was barely passable, as it was still rocky, curvy and hilly. It was roughly brushed out, leaving it very narrow and closely flanked by forest.

Settlers soon began to complain as drovers and immigrants camped along the roads due to a lack of available accommodations. Poorly attended fires often spread to roadsides and bridges, causing significant damage.

In 1824, it was petitioned and accepted to change the road from the west side of the Kennebec to the east side. The east side was more suitable for building, already boasting small settlements, and this would encourage more.

The hopeful travelers, tired, hungry, and out of money, stopped to find shelter in these small settlements. Some worked for their keep while some decided to settle in that community. Others would continue on to mill towns in Maine, Massachusetts or Rhode Island.

There were Irishmen in 1828 traveling south from Canada on their way to the land of liberty. Many having been on the trail were starving by the time they reached The Forks. Smith, who owned and operated the ferry at The Forks, must either ferry them across or "keep" them all for free.

Tramps, creating fear of thievery, fires, and the molesting of young persons, continued to camp alongside the roads and villages, such as The Forks village.

Chapter 3

THE FORKS PLANTATION: EARLY HISTORY

ON THE 1820 Map of Maine by Moses Greenleaf and engraver, William B. Annin, The Forks, including the area which we now know as "Hangtown", is in No.1 or T1 Range 4 of Bingham's Kennebec Purchase. Consisting of 39.6 square miles of land and 1.9 square miles of water equaling 41.5 square miles, it became organized on November 2, 1840.

John Black, in 1820, reported that there were no permanent settlers at The Forks. Although the 1820 U.S. Federal Census shows Tracia Howe living in the area north of Caratunk. It appears he soon left the area after being convicted of stealing, and was sentenced to serve time in prison. Howe escaped twice on his way to prison. The second time, he was successful, and he seemed to have disappeared from succeeding The Forks' censuses.

There was a big increase in the demand for timberlands, and the decision to sell large tracts of land was more interesting to the Bingham Trustees than trying to encourage settlers with small lots. This encouraged surveys for whole townships to be drawn up and sold, excepting the land already settled. The earlier settlers would be able to purchase their land at a later date.

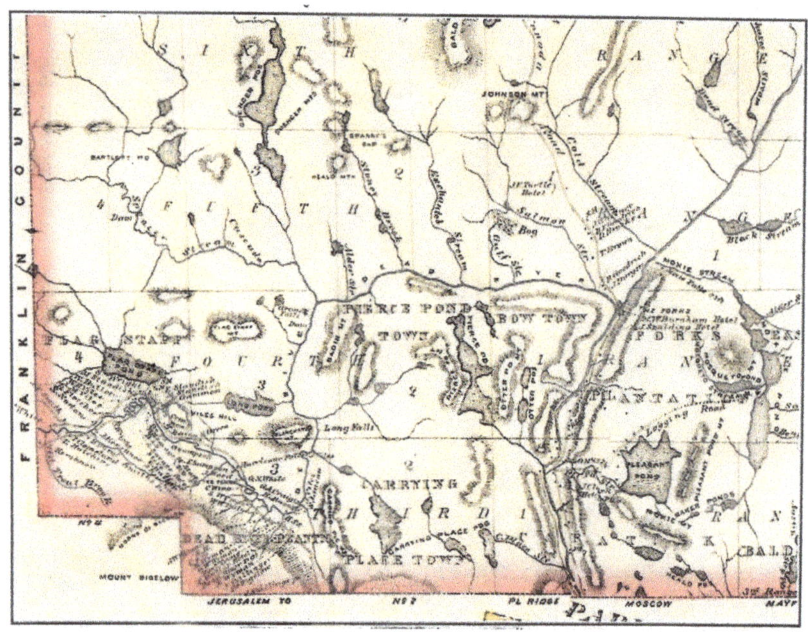

Image 2. Flagstaff and The Forks Plantation 1860

Joseph Spaulding Sr., after moving from Embden to Caratunk, opened a hotel in 1816. At the time there were only four rooms and no plumbing, and, of course, no electricity. It was called The Hotel at Caratunk and was also a stagecoach stop on the Canada Road. The Canada Road was the main route between Quebec and the Atlantic Ocean.

[The Hotel at Caratunk later became known as the Webster Inn, and later Hotel Sterling in 1910. Today it is known as The Sterling Hotel. Spaulding sold to Joseph Clark and stayed in the Clark family until Ralph Sterling, a great-grandson of Clark, took over, renaming it from the Webster Inn to the Hotel Sterling. Today it is known as the Sterling Inn and owned by Matt Polstein.]

In 1820, B.B. Boise had a building at Parlin Pond with food and drink, where travelers could spend the night. This further encouraged settlements in the area. Settlers traveling south or north no longer needed to camp alongside the road, as long as they had money or ambition to work. Tramps were a problem, for they arrived with no money, would not work for money or their keep, but expected hand-outs– often stealing when not accommodated. Some locals feared they were bringing the plague with them as well.

Cholera in 1832 caused around 6,000 people to die in Canada and two years later cholera struck again. Small Pox 1885 in Canada; typhus in 1659 and in 1847, 9293 immigrants, particularly Irish descent, died. In 1918 to 1819, 50,000 Canadians were lost to the Spanish Flu and Influenza. No wonder the settlers were so apprehensive.

The growth of the settlements was slow. T1 R 4 on the East side of the Kennebec (The Forks), in the 1830 census, shows seven households with a total of 25 males and 16 females. The heads of households were: Daniel Williams and brother-Jacob Williams, Laskey Kealiher, John Bumpus, Warren Bumpus, William Steward, and William Homes. The last five households were all related by marriage.

John Bradley, 51 year old farmer from Fryeburg, bought the entire T1 Range 4 E (The Forks) from John Black, the agent for the Bingham Estate Trustees, in 1832. This transaction did not include the public and settler's lots. The settlers, as promised before, would eventually get a chance to purchase their homes.

In 1840, the potato blight in Ireland and the restrictions in England on citizens, caused the Irish and English to swarm to Canada and further to Maine. Many immigrants from Canada (French, Scots, Irish, and English) were now using the Old Canada Road to bring their herds of sheep (for market); or to work in the hay and potato fields, logging, or traveling further to the mills. Whole townships were being bought up by wealthy land barons, and boom towns were springing up along the rivers and lakes, with sawmills and grist mills. The whole lumbering business was booming and needed laborers and the mills embraced the influx of immigrant workers and the growth of the settlements.

The 1840 census shows there were now settlers in the Pleasant Pond area, along with settlers listed under The Forks Plantation. The residents at the Pleasant Pond Area were James White, Jacob Emington (Emerton), Joseph Spaulding, and Enoch Webster. More heads of families were listed under The Forks Plantation No.1, 4th Range, adding Thomas M. McGuire (wife, 1 son, and 1 daughter); Thomas Berry (himself only); David S. Young (wife and 3 daughters).

By 1850, The Forks Census listed fourteen households with a total of 52 males and 46 females. There were eleven farmers listed, one blacksmith, one lumberman, nine laborers, and one milliner.

[One who designs, manufactures, and sells hats. Also used in the general sense of selling specialized clothing.]

These individuals were from parts of Maine, Massachusetts, Canada, Ireland, and England.

This brings us to the next era, which included the completion of the road on the east side of the Kennebec, making travel so much easier for all, including the stage coach!

Chapter 4

THE STAGE

Moses Hanscom of Farmington was the first stage coach driver who was contracted to deliver the mail, freight, and passengers in the area above Bingham from 1832 to 1836. The stage made two runs weekly to The Forks with a team of two to six horses pulling a covered wagon, and covered sled in the winter.

[The Forks post office opened around 1831.]

Hanscom could carry fifteen passengers along with the mail, and freight stacked on the back of the wagon. The roads were rough and the passengers could barely hold on to their seats. The early wagons had no springs to absorb the bumps until years later when leather straps were installed as springs.

There were many stage coach drivers throughout the years before velocipedes were introduced to the area. Some making harrowing trips and some with unforgettable passengers.

Gardner Sterling Benson was born in 1848. At what age he became a stage driver remains debatable. He was from Solon and drove a stage from The Forks to Moose River, (Jackman). Describing a few of his trips to The Independent Reporter in 1921, he boasts that he made the thirty mile trip from The Forks to Moose River in one day. Carrying the mail, express, and passengers, he stopped at Parlin Pond to eat dinner and change horses. He returned home the next day proudly having used only four horses.

Benson sometimes had to drive through heavy snows but never missed a trip in the two years he drove The Forks to Jackman route. If roads were impassable then the mail was carried on by snowshoes.

The next route Benson drove was from Skowhegan to The Forks. As with many of the stage coach drivers, Benson faced numerous hardships on his routes.

Dealing with heavy snows, he was on his way to Bingham and had eight more miles to go. Just south of the Carney Hotel he had to turn back due to heavy, deep snow.

[Carney Hotel, Moscow, burned in 1888-
Old Canada Road Historical Society has
a picture of the Carney Hotel.]

He stopped at the hotel, took his supper and harnessed one horse to a pung continuing his route towards Bingham, and encountered impassable snow drifts at Turner Pond. Not wanting to turn back, he guided his horse to the steep bank of the pond and found a clearing to urge his horse over. He relates how his horse sat down on his haunches and slid down onto the pond. From there Benson finally arrived in Bingham where he met other drivers heading north. Being the half-way point for the stages here, drivers would get their dinner and a change of horses then proceed on to northerly destinations. Due to the storm and blocked roads Benson and the other stage drivers had to stay in Bingham a week waiting for the roads to clear.

Most days Benson carried ten to fifteen passengers, most being lumbermen. At one time he tells us that passenger fare was as low as $1.00 from Skowhegan to The Forks. Many times he carried several thousand dollars of payroll for the lumbermen, located further north. However, he related that he was never held up!

There were other drivers like Irving Young who was Benson's alternate. Around 1889, Albert Murry, of The Forks, ran the Mail Stage from Skowhegan to Solon with tri-weekly trips to The Forks and very possibly more daily trips depending on patronage.

In 1889, the stage left Skowhegan for Norridgewock at 4 p.m., connecting with the train for Emden. From there, passengers continued by stage to Bingham, arriving at 9:30 p.m., for fare $1.25. The fare from Bingham to The Forks was $1.25, and from The Forks to Moose River was $2.00. The stage leaving Bingham daily at 7 a.m., with dinner at The Forks, and overnight at Parlin Pond, reached Moose River at noon of the second day. The entire trip from Skowhegan to Moose River cost $4.50 and two nights on the road.

Another stagecoach driver, William Whorff, held the mail contract somewhere around 1893 to 1943. He was born in 1873 to Charles and Jane Whorff of Bingham. He later married Nancy A. McCollar and they raised four children. Nancy was the great-granddaughter of Patrick McCollar, who made that journey from St. George, Canada, to Bingham, Maine, earlier in 1815.

Whorff was a U.S. Mail Carrier who lived in Bingham until 1910. He then moved to the "Jackman Road", Caratunk. Along with being the mail carrier, he owned interest in Pierce Pond Sporting Camps located north on the Old Canada Road. He turned his own home into an inn for tourists waiting to continue their journey on to the Pierce Pond Camps or further north.

The Forks stage was the only means of conveyance to all the towns above Skowhegan for years. It was replaced with automobiles around 1912. William Whorff finishing out his career with automobiles retired in 1943.

Back in 1851, Maine was the first state to make it illegal to manufacture and sell liquor (unless it was for medicinal, mechanical and manufacturing purposes). It did not halt the ability to obtain liquor nor the consuming of it. There was much "rum running" during the five years it was law.

There was a colorful character driving the route from The Forks to Moxie Station who was often in trouble with the law. Specifically in the early months of 1909 when he, Warren Durgin, was victim to search and seizure by Sheriff Moore's deputies, Perley Foss of Bingham and John Foss of Solon. A few weeks later he was charged with a single sale action. He was convicted on the single sale, fined $50 and costs, taxed at $10.00 in addition to 30 days in jail. On conviction for maintaining a liquor nuisance.

[A liquor nuisance was defined as the act of
having an intoxicating liquor business.]

---

he was fined $100 and costs; taxed $10, and 60 days in jail with an additional 60 days if the fine and costs were not paid.

What a laugh Warren Durgin must have had when a few months later Sheriff Moores dispatched eight deputies to serve and execute search warrants in Jackman and Moose River. Two automobiles were employed for the purpose with four deputies in each. They left Skowhegan in the early morning and somewhere between Bingham and Caratunk the rear axle of one vehicle broke, dropping the occupants into the road! These deputies returned to Skowhegan via a team. The second car continued on to Jackman. When returning, as they passed The Forks, a cone in the engine broke and there they sat very near to the residence of the notorious, Warren Durgin! Mr. Durgin hitched up his team and kindly took the deputies to Bingham!

As the railway extended to Caratunk Falls and beyond, Skowhegan, once the major terminal center for both trains and stages, bowed to the railroads marking the end to many stage lines.

Chapter 5

THE RAILROAD 1872–1904

THERE WERE 31 railroad lines operating in Maine between the years of 1842 and 1906.

The Somerset Railroad was completed in stages: It started at the Maine Central Railroad "back road" at Oakland continuing to North Anson from 1872–1877. Norridgewock, Madison, and North Anson spent $30,000 per mile building the track. After defaulting in 1879, it was reorganized as the standard gauge Somerset Railway in 1884. By 1890, the tracks had reached Solon and Bingham. Many of the workers were Italian, as McDougall writes.

[Walter M. McDougall, The Old Somerset Railroad, Down East Books, Camden, Maine, page 63.]

He adds that many Italian workers' bodies were lying in unmarked graves in Bingham. Italians were known for their love of bread and drink. The workers were often intoxicated and unable to work or did work that resulted in accidents. Henry Hill, a civil engineer, laid out plans for the tracks from Bingham to Moxie Pond in 1904.

Rails began to be laid from Bingham north to carry both freight and passengers, known as a mixed train. This was a huge benefit to the hotels, sporting camps located in The Forks, Lake Parlin, Upper Enchanted Township and others. By 1906, the tracks ran to the foot of Moxie Lake and then north nine miles along Moxie Lake and reached Moosehead Lake in 1906. Some of the trains were now running on coal instead of wood.

A station house built in Moxie was six miles from The Forks. A road already existed between Moxie and The Forks Village. Rather than mail being delivered to Bingham and then transported twenty-three miles by stage to The Forks, the train dropped the mail at Moxie Station for the six-mile stage delivery to The Forks.

There were "flagging stations" where red flags were left at various locations. Those who wanted to board the train would wave the flag to stop the train. As many did when they took a trip to Waterville to see the Barnum & Bailey Circus- and at one such time to see Jess Willard's boxing match. Willard, born in 1881, was 6 feet 6 ½ inches tall. He was known as the Pottawatomie Giant. Ida Crotto Allen, from Moxie, was one who traveled to see him.

Willard in 1915, won the heavyweight title in boxing, knocking out Jack Johnson and held that title for four years. Out of thirty-four fights, he only lost seven. Twenty of his wins were knock outs.

[A must read: ida by Ardelle "ida" Allen,
The Thorndike Press, 1979.]

The train brought many benefits to the citizens and was vital to increasing the transporting of logs, lumber and many other products from the northern woods. Items like hardwood could now be shipped via rail because these hardwood logs would not float like softwood and were left out of the log drives.

Lake Moxie Station was where some passengers heading north disembarked. Residents, loggers, lumbermen, sportsmen, including celebrities, continued their travels by horse drawn carriages, wagons, stages, on foot or on horseback. They, traveled not just to The Forks, but Upper Enchanted Township, Lake Parlin, and other remote destinations further north along the Canada road.

By 1916, the train ticket sales were decreasing. In 1881, nearly 802 tickets were sold by a station agent to those traveling to see the circus that year in Waterville. In 1916 there were only 227 passenger tickets sold at the same station for transportation to the circus that year. The decline in ticket sales was most likely connected to the increased production of automobiles now used for travel.

On March 11, 1929, the Somerset Railway was discontinued—but not until 1936 did they start removing the tracks. The Japanese bought the rails for junk metal.

The Maine Central Railroad was still in operation and much needed for transporting pulpwood.

Using swollen freshet rivers in the spring, pulpwood was floated down the Kennebec River to Wyman Dam, where it was loaded onto the Maine Central Railroad in Bingham. Some of the logs may have continued south down the Kennebec River to the paper mills.

The log drives on the Kennebec and its tributaries were quite a process. Logs were hauled by teams of oxen or horses and then by log haulers such as the Lombard hauler to the banks of streams from the timber country. With the rise of the streams, men known as, "River Pigs" or "River Rats" were hired to push these logs into the streams and drive them to the Log Driving Corporation. The local one was the Kennebec Log Driving Company or KLD.

[Check out Wallingford's Inc, You Tube video
"Logging 1950's West Forks, Me."]

The Log Driving Corporation was a company formed by interested parties in lumbering in a specific section, district, or area. It was established for the mutual benefit of all lumbermen and was authorized by the Legislature of the State of Maine. The pollution caused by the bark lying on the bottom, log hazards floating around rivers and lakes damaging boats, and the paper mills dumping sludge into the rivers and streams prompted the passage of the Clean Water Act of 1972. The fact that the Golden Road which is a ninety-six-mile private-stone-and-gravel road between Millinocket, Maine, through the Maine North Woods, to St. Zacharie Border Crossing, was completed that same year, only contributed to the end of the log drives in Maine. The end of a typical timbering era and the bowing out of trains. A new era with trucking began.

No longer would River Drivers, River Pigs. booms, peaveys, cant dogs, and caulks be household words. The River Pigs, cursing and singing as they guided the logs down raging rivers to mills, were replaced by smelly diesel-powered tractor-trailers hauling the logs. Those trucks, loudly shifting gears up and down the long hills, and eventually with their Jake Brakes waking all as the trucks slowed for towns, replaced the clinking of iron on rails and the long eerie whistles of trains. A new era indeed.

CHAPTER 6

EARLY SETTLERS OF THE PLEASANT POND AREA

PLEASANT POND IS in The Town of Caratunk and in The Forks Plantation. There were early settlers around Pleasant Pond T1 R3 (Caratunk) by 1835. By 1840 in (T1R4) The Forks Plantation there were four settlers with families living in the Pleasant Pond area. Enoch Webster, Jacob Emerton, Joseph White, and Joseph Spaulding were the first settlers, with the population increasing by 1845. Enoch Webster, by 1845, had sold his property to Joseph Spaulding and he, three months later, sold to Robert Love, who, by 1845, was already a resident of Pleasant Pond, The Fork's. The deed description identifies it as the same premises that Love's father and family were living near Pleasant Pond.

Jacob Emerton was only listed in the 1840 census of The Forks, in the Pleasant Pond area. When researching Emerton, very little was revealed of his presence at Pleasant Pond. He was born in 1811 in Columbia, N.H., and later moved to Moscow, Maine. He was married to Susan and their children were Thomas, Susannah, John, Andrew,

Elvira, Rachael, Amos, and Clara. Emerton's lot in T1R4 East of the Kennebec was purchased from the Coburns in 1857 and appears to have been used as his backlot, meaning he did not live there. Eventually it is owned by a paper company, Umbagog.

[Umbagog was founded in 1881 by Hugh Chisholm, Livermore Falls. His mill produced heavy wrapping and board papers. Sometimes used for bottle caps and lining caskets.]

Joseph White was 40 years old, his wife 20, and 2 young daughters under 5, when listed in The Forks 1840 census. Further censuses did not list him. I could find no further information on him. I did find a Joseph White, farmer, in Madison in 1820(s) census. Their ages would be correct but no further evidence that this was the same Joseph White.

Joseph Spaulding Jr, was a prominent citizen of Caratunk. However, he was listed as a resident of The Forks Plantation at Pleasant Pond, 1840 census. He obtained many acres of land, divided it into lots, and sold these to settlers, while also offering large tracks of timberland to lumbermen.

[A short history of Joseph Spaulding Jr. can be found in Donna McAllister's The Sesquicentennial History of Caratunk, Maine; printed by Carrabassett Printers, North Anson, Maine.]

By 1850, Robert Love, having bought the Webster lot from Joseph Spaulding, was the head of household on his farm in The Forks' Pleasant Pond area. Living with him are his parents, John and Elizabeth, his wife, Clarissa, and baby Elizabeth Jane.

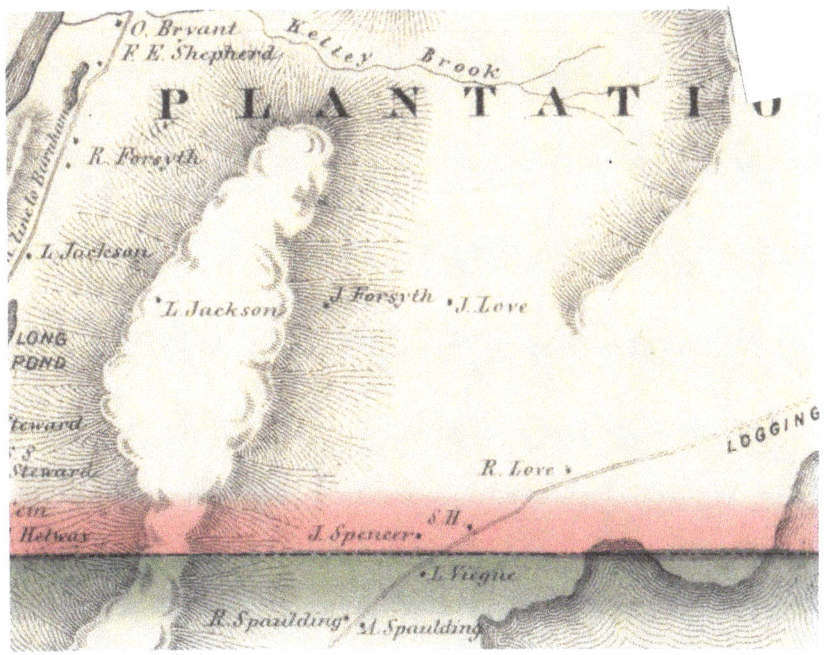

Image 3. Early settlers in the Pleasant Pond area, 1860

By 1860, they had eight children living in their household-Elizabeth Jane, Davis, Willis, Robard (Robert), John, Clara, Willie Livingston, and Mary Livingston.

The 1860 Chase map of Somerset County shows evidence of two additional farms, John Love's and John Forsyth's. Neither of these men are listed in censuses following 1860.

By 1864, Robert Love was a private in the Civil War with Co. G, 31st infantry and was wounded at Petersburg, Virginia. Soon after returning home, he sold to John Carny from Moscow. In 1865, Carny sold the Robert Love Lot to Albert Spaulding.

I have used two maps to describe the following lots:

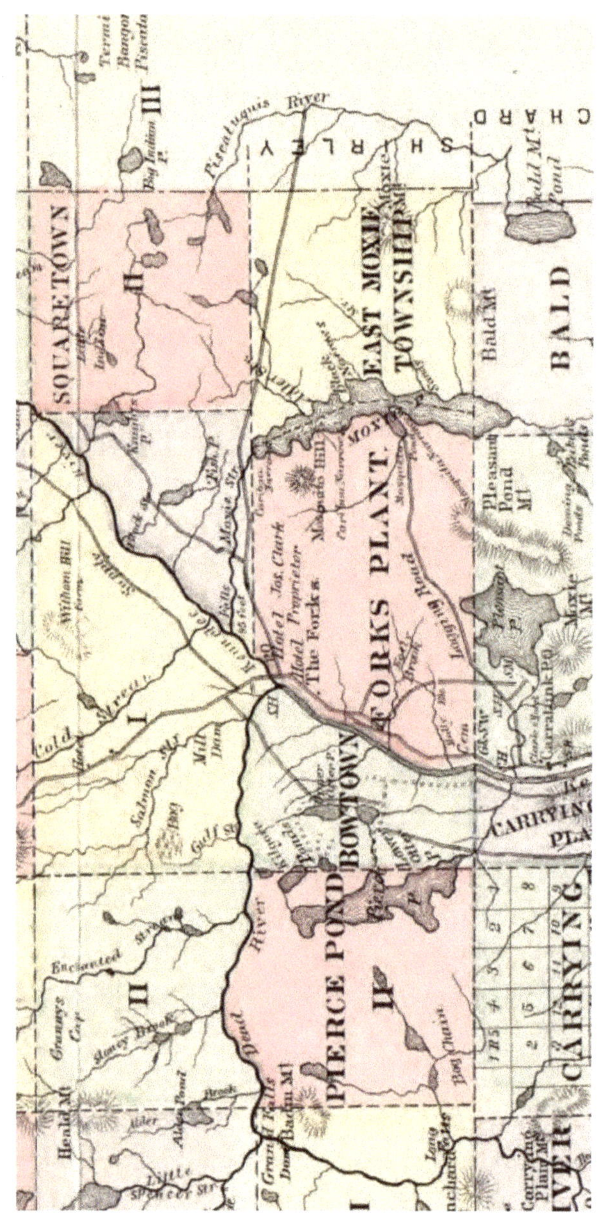

Image 4. G. N. Colby's 1883 Map of Maine—
South section of The Forks Plantation.

Albert C. Spaulding, born to Richard and Susan Spaulding in 1842, owned the Lot #28 shown on the Colby 1903 map.

Albert's residence in 1870 was at Pleasant Pond, The Forks Plantation.

By now, the term 'Pleasant Ponders' referred to the settlement of those farms on the Pleasant Pond Road. Spaulding purchased this land from the Heirs of Josheph Clark in 1888. It straddled the boundary between Caratunk and The Forks. Newspapers referred to him as being from Pleasant Pond.

Albert was a farmer and lumberman. Abutting his land to the north was Justus Adams. Bordering his land on the south side of the Pond road and to his west was his brother, Barrett Spaulding. Barrett's farm abutted Pleasant Pond Stream. To his east was Cyrus Williams.

Albert married Sarah W. Bean in 1875. They had a total of twelve children. A son at the age of 5 died in 1888, and another ten month old child died in 1896. Their children: Jennie, Delmont, Annie, Perley, Eugene, Alice, George, Elsie, Sadie, and Ralph, lived to be adults. However, Ralph was killed during World War I on February 13, 1918, in France. He was only twenty-one.

Albert Spaulding moved his family to Emden in 1900 where he continued to farm and work in the woods. In 1909, the same year his brother Barrett died, Albert sold his Pleasant Pond farm to Fred Clark and Nathaniel Brown. His wife, Sarah, died in 1917 from chronic interstitial nephritis. Albert died five years later from stomach cancer.

The Spaulding Farm became known as the Maude Clark Farm and today is owned by the Bateman's.

Cyrus P. Williams' lot is on the east side of Spaulding's as shown on the 1883 map published by the Geo. N. Colby. It is displayed as #27 on the 1903 Forest Colby Map.

Cyrus' parents, Francis and Nancy Williams, settled this property before 1840. He is on the 1840 and 1850 census. They raised a large family: Atwell R, Harriet H, Clarissa H who later married Robert

Love, Charles W, Horace S, Jason P, Leonard H, Nancy J, Francis L, Jr., Cyrus P, and Lewis K.

Cyrus married Susan Cordelia "Delia" Spaulding. They had two children Fred and Nellie V. and later married Mike Kennedy. By 1870, Cyrus was residing in Bingham. Over the years, as with many farms, it was sold, mortgaged, foreclosed on, and sold again.

In 1886, Mike Kennedy bought it from Omar Clark et al, the heirs of Joseph Clark. Kennedy sold to lumberman Henry Lovejoy in 1887. While holding the mortgage, Lovejoy sold the property to Cyrus' son Fred in 1891. This was followed by foreclosure in 1894. A man named Parris lived there between 1896 and 1897. Then Baker bought and mortgaged with Lovejoy from 1897 to 1899, reserving his right to live there. This ended with a foreclosure as well. Finally in 1900, Henry Lovejoy sold it to Mrs. W. B. (Alice) Goodrich of Bingham, and Frank Taylor.

On Spaulding's north boundary, Justus Adams owned lot #33, which encompassed 160 acres. It was occasionally referred to as the Jesse Adams lot.

Born in Caratunk in 1824, Justus was the son of William Adams II. In 1852, he worked in Caratunk with Richard Spaulding.

Justus was enlisted as a private in H 1st Heavy Artillery, at the age of thirty-nine. He was wounded in Petersburg June 18, 1864, after serving fourteen months. He was discharged from Cony Hospital, Augusta, on January 14, 1865 with disability.

Justus married Albert's sister, Mary A. Spaulding. Their children were: Amos born in 1866, Eveline in 1868, Says (who died young), and George born in 1870.

The 1880 Non-Population Census shows Justus Adams was farming with 160 acres valued at $385.00, and with farm income of $175.00. He had harvested 6 tons of hay, 160 bushels of potatoes, and 125 pounds of butter. His farm did not seem to be as productive as some of the others listed.

Justus mortgaged his homestead to Oren Vittum, in 1882, and Vittum foreclosed on him the next year.

I found no evidence of when Justus left Pleasant Pond. However, in 1890, he, along with his son, bought two hundred and twenty acres in Solon from Abel Rowell.

Evidently, Adams' wife, Mary, left him sometime later in 1897. At that time, he published a notice stating that she had left with no cause and that he would not be responsible for any debts.

Justus Adams experienced a shock in September 1901. Later, in 1902, he was reported sick at B. S. Kincaid's and having been so for the last few months. On July 16, 1902 he left Solon being admitted to the Soldier's Home at Chelsea, and died four days later. He was 78.

Omar Clark, and William H. Clark, quite the land barons, eventually, acquired the Justus/Jesse Adams lot. Years later, Omar was determined to be a person of unsound mind. William Clark, Omar's Guardian, and nine others sold the Justus 'Jesse' Adams lot to the lumberman, Alanson Hunnewell, in September of 1921.

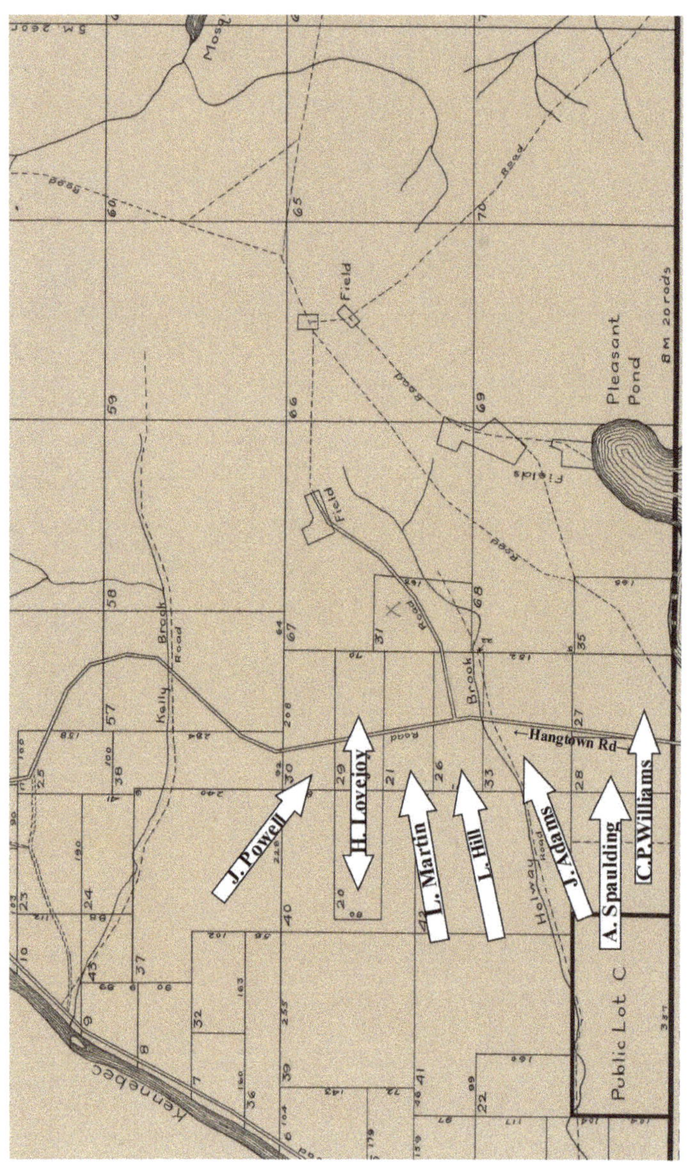

Image 5. Forest Colby's 1903 Survey of Maine settlers lot No(s).

Chapter 7

HANGTOWN AREA'S EARLY SETTLERS

As SETTLEMENTS GREW along the Kennebec River, settlers moved further inland for farming and closer to timberland. A neighborhood of farms, later becoming known as Hangtown, was established further north of Pleasant Pond.

Late in the 1870s, Abner Coburn and Heirs of Philander Coburn, owned many acres of T1R4. For Seven Thousand Eight Hundred Dollars they sold many parcels (excepting the settler's lots), to Joseph Clark, a lumberman. In turn, Joseph Clark started selling 100 acre lots north of Pleasant Pond and Holly Brook. These lots would eventually make up Hangtown. Henry Lovejoy, a farmer and logging operation's owner, bought two lots #20 and #29 in 1879 and settled there. Lewis Martin bought his lot #21 in 1879 as well. Miriam and Lawrence Hill bought their lot #26 in 1882, and already settled on lot #30, was James Powell Jr., struggling for existence.

By 1880, ambitious settlers were carving out an existence in the rocky soil along a rough trail north from Pleasant Pond. Among these determined settlers was James E. Powell, Jr., a child survivor of the Civil War who arrived in the 1870s. He later became a successful farmer, woodsman, and a resident of what eventually became Hangtown in The Forks Plantation.

James E. Powell Jr., was the oldest son of James E. Powell and Mary Ann (Hunter) Powell. His father was born in England and his mother was born in English Canada. James Jr. was born in The Forks, Maine on June 30, 1850. At the age of five, young James left Maine with his father, who had joined the U.S. Regular Army on December 5, 1856. James' mother and his two younger brothers, Winfield Scott, born in 1853, and Albert Tracy, born on October 20, 1855, remained behind. James father was commissioned as first lieutenant, and as was common practice at the time, James became his father's waiter during the Civil War.

[Definition of waiter-in the military is a
young boy who assists or aides to another's
needs, most usually their father.]

Powell, in June of 1861, was made Captain with the 25th Missouri Volunteers. On March 24, 1862 he was given the title of Brevet Major. He was mustered out on April 6, 1862 at Shiloh, Pittsburg Landing, and Harden County, Tennessee. On April 6, 1862, around 1 pm, James E. Powell Sr. was mortally wounded and died that night.

Six days prior to his death, Powell responded to a letter from his ex-wife, Mary—she had divorced him, two years prior. Here is a response to that letter, found at Fold3.com.

Army of West Tennessee

March 31st, 1862

Mary,

By the merest accident in the world I received your letter. I am very glad to hear that Win and Tracy are well, and good little fellows. I should very much like to see them.

Give my love to them and tell them that I don't forget them.

It is very easy indeed to find fault.—I have got no money. I have not had any for some time.

We are now in front of the enemy near the Alabama line, and provided I live through the coming fights I will send you money as soon as I get it.—That may be two months yet!

Jimmy is with me. He sends his love to you and Win and Tracy. — I cannot tell when I shall write again. The difficulties of sending letters is very great here at present. When I get pay, then I shall write.

—I congratulate you. Jim sends his love to the baby! –Yours

J.E. Powell

—Source: Fold3.com, Civil War Letters Collection, accessed December 2021]

As previously mentioned, Powell died in action just six days after this letter was written.

Knowing the uncertainty of his health or life, Powell had made prior arrangements with a friend, Captain E. W. Dimock, to see that young James was cared for. After Powell's death, Captain Dimock reached out to his father in Newark, N.J., seeking assistance in locating James family and arranging for the boy's care until they could be found.

When asked about his early home life, young James only remembered the name Burnham and that Burnham owned a hotel.

Burnham's hotel was known as The Forks Hotel which he had bought in 1836 from Lemuel Fletcher— previously built and owned by E.G. Sturgis in 1833.

Moses Burnham was an aggressive land purchaser. He was a much respected business man, and was one of the major players in the Moosehead Lake Steam Navigation Company of 1835.

[Mid 1800s steam navigation allowed for better transportation of people, mail, supplies, and more to farms, camps, businesses, and so on. Development of roads and automobiles in the late 1930s ended this use of the steamboat. Later they were used as towboats for hauling booms or rafts of logs.]

Burnham owned a vast amount of property including a hotel, tavern, stores, blacksmith shop and he held many mortgages for the early settlers in The Forks. He was also postmaster in 1836. There had been a dispute between Burnham and young James' father. The 'Sheriff's Judgement' settled in Burnham's favor with Powell losing his remaining possessions by 1856. Perhaps this is why James' father had left the area. However, Moses Burnham was not at The Forks in 1862 when at the age of twelve, young James was finally reunited with his mother and brothers.

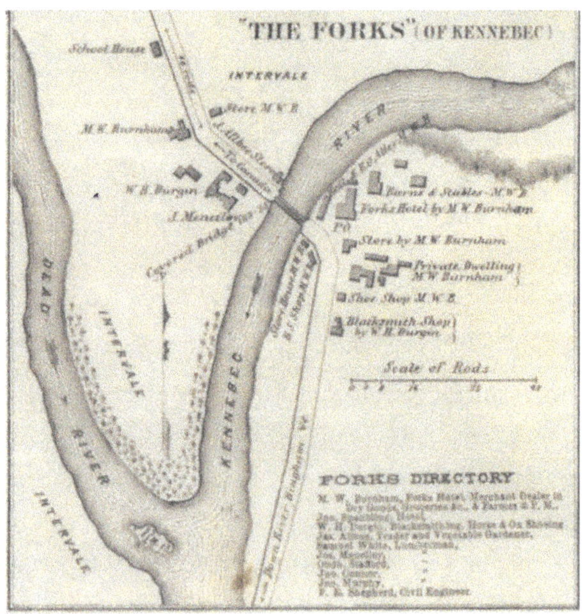

Image 6. G. N Colby's 1860 Burnham's Lot.

Moses Burnham had left The Forks rather suddenly in 1861, soon after an Irishman shepherd, Mitchel Berry, was found dead. He was working for Burnham at the time of his death. Berry, with a rope around his neck and the other end tied to an empty, but holed bag, was found washed up on the riverbank at Bingham. Burnham and a man from Solon named Vickery was suspected of foul play, but it appears they were never charged with the crime. Soon after, Burnham sold all his property by September 1861, and was gone from The Forks.

[In 1861, Joseph Clark, Jr. and Philander Coburn bought all of Moses Burnham's Upper Kennebec Property which included the old Spaulding's Hotel, with Burnham's exit out of Maine. Joseph Clark Jr. had moved to Caratunk in 1854 and owned 150,000 acres of timberland at his death. It was valued at 50 cents per acre. —The Forks Hotel burned in 1906.]

With only the name Burnham for reference, on August 5, 1862 Dimock's father, reached out to the State of Maine's Governor Washburn to help in the search of James' family. Capt. Dimock also mentioned to his own father that the boy and his family should receive a pension from Powell Sr.'s service to the country.

Mary applied for a pension but was refused because she had remarried. It was after James Jr. was reunited with his mother and brothers, that Mary tried again filing under her three son's names. It took some time and a lot of paperwork but finely Powell's boys were granted a pension on March 31, 1863 and retroactive to the day their father died.

When young James' mother, Mary Ann, divorced his father in 1860, she married Obadiah Stafford, who was a farm laborer for Jonathan Spaulding.

[Spaulding was listed in the statistics of 1850 on the
1860 Map of Somerset County as "Lumberman"
under the Forks Directory on that map. Spaulding's
farm today would be on the west side of the
Hangtown Road near the intersection.]

It was Stafford and Mary's baby that Powell had referred to in his letter. Stafford died three years later, 1866, and Mary's son, Albert Tracy, age fourteen, died in 1869. Mary's third marriage was to William Adams, a farmer. He was only eight years older than James.

[Mary is found in Adams' household in 1870 census
with Stafford's and her daughter, five year old
Matilda, and Mary's son, Winfield Powell who is now
16 and a farm laborer; also, two of Adams' and her
children: William (3) and Lizzie J. (1)].] James must be
seventeen and is not listed in Adams' household.]

Where James lived between 1866 and 1870 is unknown to the author. He appears again in the 1870 The Forks' census with the John B. Adams household. He is listed as a farm worker. Adams was a farmer, who previously (1860 census) lived and farmed in Bowtown and in the 1870's, he has moved, and farming in The Forks Plantation.

[John Adams family: wife was Zalpha and
children: Nathan 10, Phebe 9, and George 2]

James married Lizzie Turner Bates in 1870. They soon became residents of The Forks Plantation living at what is known today as Hangtown. Powell's farm was on lot #30 prior to 1895.

James and Lizzie proceeded to raise a large family on their farm. Their son, Tracy, was born in 1872, Mary in 1873, David Eugene in 1875, James Edwin in 1877, and Evelyn 'Eva' in 1880.

He, along with his neighbors, were working their farms during the growing season for sustainment and income, along with working for logging operations

To give a sense of what farms were producing, Powell was listed in the U.S. Selected Census Non-Population Schedule of 1880, based on the 1879 harvest, as having 45 acres of improved land and 100 acres unimproved. James Powell had 40 acres of hay producing 23 tons. 1 Acre of Buckwheat produced 15 bushels; 1/3 acre of Indian corn produced 15 bushels; ¾ acre of oats produced 25 bushels and 1 acre of wheat produced 21 bushels. Pulse- Canada Peas (dry) 3 bushels and Beans (dry) 4 bushels. He had 2 acres in potatoes which produced 350 bushels; ¼ acre with 5 apple trees produced 6 bushels of apples.

He also had 1 horse, 2 working oxen, 3 milk cows, and 7 'other,' 1 Swine, 20 poultry and 200 dozen eggs produced. He had 44 sheep with 16 lambs dropped, 3 slaughtered and 44 fleeces which weighed 176 pounds. Some farmers produced Maple Sugar but Powell showed none for this period. In forest products he cut 14 cords of wood and sold $28.00 worth. The value of his farm was $1100: $100 in equipment and $400 in livestock. It appears his cost of producing income of $325.00 was $103.00.

The Powells were not the only ones who lived in this area in 1879. Land was being sold in 100-acre lots. Their neighbors going south towards Pleasant Pond were David Devoll, Henry Lovejoy, Lewis Marten, Lawrence Hill, and beyond Holly Brook, Justus Adams, Albert Spaulding and Cyrus Williams.

[The 1883 map also shows Thomas Emerton (his father, Jacob, had passed away), and Clark with property east of Hill's, Lovejoy's, and Martin's homesteads. Neither Emerton nor Clark seems to have resided on their land.]

Chapter 8

HANGTOWN NEIGHBORS

THE LOVEJOYS WERE residents of The Forks Plantation from 1879-1889, and the Devolls from 1879-1888. In 1879, Henry Lovejoy bought two 100 acre lots, (#s 20 and 29) from Joseph Clark. He and wife, Julia G. (Devoll) Lovejoy, their 5 children, Frank, Nellie, Emma, Herbert, Orion, and Julia's daughter (from a previous marriage), Myrtia Cleveland,

---

[Later they were to have two more
children, Blanche and Lula.]

---

moved to their new homestead from Athens. Lovejoy had resided in Athens for twenty years, during which he built the farm buildings on the Wilson Wells farm. At The Forks, he built his new homestead where he farmed and logged. He owned a complete outfit including, two horses and two oxen. The area was already well-known for its logging activities.

In 1880, his new farm, on the east side of the woods trail, (Hangtown Road), according to the U.S. Non-Population was valued at $975, ($600 in land, fences, and buildings, $25 in farm equipment, and $350 in livestock). He had 3 milk cows, 1 other, 19 sheep, 12 lambs, 1 swine, 5 hens and 2 cattle. He had produced in 1879, 200 pounds of butter, 133 pounds of fleece, 50 dozen eggs, 20 tons of hay, and 15 cord of wood.

Lovejoy's second lot, #20, was west of his homestead. It was this lot that David Devoll (Julia's brother) and his family moved in 1879. Devoll's farm, appraised at $225, was considered slightly below average on the 1880 Non-Population Census. He had 1 milk cow, 3 other; he sold 17 lambs. He produced 100 bushel of potatoes, 475 pounds of butter, 360 bushels of oats, 8 bushels of buckwheat, and cut 12 cords of wood. David Devoll never owned the land.

Devoll's wife was Olive B. (Young) and they had six children- Julia, Mary, Charles, Lilla, Hattie, Seth, and Perley. It was soon after Perley was born, in 1888, when the Devolls left and moved to Skowhegan. He went on to be an Evangelist.

It was the next year after Devoll left, when Henry Lovejoy moved to Caratunk. Later, he moved to Moscow where he became a prominent citizen. In 1891, he sold his farm and 200 acres (lots # 20 and #29) to William Adams (James Powell's step-father). In 1894, he sold lot #30 to Henry Prince. Lovejoy's presence was no longer in Hangtown and The Forks! Being a woodsman to the core, Lovejoy continued logging until he was eighty-three.

On Lovejoy's southern border was Lewis Martin's farm on lot #21. He was a resident of The Forks Plantation from 1879 to 1890.

Martin's wife was Mary Jane (Routh) Martin. Their daughters were Nancy, Cora and Minnie.

Martin's farm was on the west side of the woods trail. It was listed on the 1880 Non-Population census with 40 acres of pasture, 35 acres of orchards & vineyards, and 25 acres of woodland. It was producing 32 tons of hay; 22 bushels of barley, and 130 bushels of oats. He owned two oxen and one milk cow. His farm was appraised for $440.

Martin, a good carpenter, moved to Caratunk by 1890 where he had built a new house. Two more children, Carroll and Ruth were born by 1894.

[The 1890 Census was destroyed by fire but further information which came from old newspaper articles definitely places Martin in Caratunk by 1894. According to Caratunk home news, Martin was getting ice and fitting the shop he rented from Robert Berry with plans to set up business. Another later article stated that Martin owned a confectionary store in Caratunk which Frank Carter leased and took possession of after Martin became ill.]

After the tragic loss of his daughter, Cora Belle, to typhoid complicated by pneumonia in 1897, Martin endured a ten-month illness before passing away on March 10, 1898. [According to the Somerset Reporter article on March 10, 1898 Martin died of la grippe and slow fever terminating in consumption.

[Scarlett Fever was also prominent in 1898]

He was just forty-two years old and left his wife, Mary (age forty), with six children, according to the newspapers. Martin Lewis is buried in the Caratunk Village Cemetery.

[I could only find five of her children: Nancy, Cora, Carroll, Minnie, Ruth. There is more confusion: Ruth's birth certificate noted she was the 7th child.]

The Martin family seems to have broken apart after Lewis' death, as Minnie is boarding with Elijah and Nancy Hall in Caratunk. Carroll was nine years old when his father died, and was adopted by James Stewart from The Forks. Nancy later married Fred Moore from

Caratunk, and Carroll was living with them in 1910. Their mother, Mary J. Martin, married Herbert Prince in June 1899 and took five-year-old Ruth with her. Mary J. (Routh), (Martin), Prince died two years later in 1901 of pelvic cancer.

James Martin (Lewis' brother) sold the Hangtown property in 1895 to Walter Prince.

[The description of the boundaries was North by James Powell, East and West by William Clark and South by Lawrence Hill]

Eventually, it became property of Walter's son, Herbert Prince, who sold it to William E. Sizeland in 1898. Sizeland's history will be discussed at a later date.

Martin's neighbor south of him was Lawrence Hill. Hill was born in Smithfield in 1853. He married Miriam S. (Cleaves), Russell. She was twenty-five years his senior and also from Smithfield. She was formally married to Sumner Russell and they had six children, Ella, Laroy, Rose, Albert, Julia and Benjamin.

When she and Lawrence moved to The Forks in 1879, only the two youngest children, Julia and Benjamin, went with them.

Hill's property was the 100-acre lot #26, sectioned by Holly Brook, as shown on the 1880 map and later in 1903 F.N. Colby Survey. Their home was on the east side, north of Holly Brook Bridge.

A beautiful rock foundation outlines what once was a very large home, with rose bushes fighting for space in overgrown fields; such a scene can still be found in 2025.

The value of Hill's farm was $900 in 1880. He had 2 horses, 2 milk cows, 13 other, 3 calves, 2 cattle sold, 14 sheep /producing 103 pounds of fleece, 7 lambs, 1 swine, 13 barnyard hens/producing 125 dozen eggs, and 15 tons of hay, 100 bushel of potatoes, and 12 cord of wood.

Hill, along with other homesteaders, did not hesitate long to petition the County Commissioner for a new county road to access their farms. On January 14, 1882, the township was assessed and a sum set for building the new county road as described in Hill and the other's petition of 1879.

The following was published in the Daily Kennebec journal (January 14, 1882):

And now on the 29th day of December, 1881 it is ordered, that there be assessed the following described township in said county of Somerset, the sum set against said township, for the purpose of making and opening a County road as laid out by the County Commissioners of said County of Somerset on petition of Lawrence P. Hill and others in 1879, in The Forks Plantation.

Hill was authorized, by the County Commissioner, to collect taxes for the road. Today, this road is known as the Hangtown Road and is discussed later in Chapter 12.

The southern end of Lawrence Hill's property is where the Hangtown school house was located. Maps indicate the school was on the east side of the road between Holly Brook and another small stream. I will talk about the school later in Chapter 9.

After settling, Hill marked out 1.5 acres for his brother-in-law, Seldon James Melvin, to homestead.

Melvin was born in 1851 in Monticello. In 1893, he, a section foreman in Bingham, married Bertha B. Hill, Lawrence's younger sister by nineteen years. Seldon later went by his middle name, James. He and Bertha had two sons, Leland M. and Walter H., and a stepdaughter, Nina Dyer. James farmed on a small scale but mainly worked in the woods. As with many, he was a good marksman, as reported by the Somerset Reporter, in the March 28, 1901 issue:

James Melvin . . . shot a loup-cervier (Canada lynx) in his field, hitting the animal with a rifle bullet between the eyes at quite a distance. The Furred skin is now at Mark Savage's and is one of the finest specimens seen for years in this region.

This region also sported an abundance of moose, deer, caribou, bobcat, and black bear.

After his request for a road to connect his farm to the existing road was denied by the County Commissioner in 1901, Melvin immediately turned to The Forks Plantation for support, but without results.

This request may have originated from his arduous horseback journey to Bingham, where his brother Basil had been struck by lightning.

August 1901, Basil Melvin and three other railroad workers were racing towards Houghton's barn for shelter from a violent storm. As they were crossing under a telephone wire, Basil was struck by lightning and killed. His co-worker, William McCuller, was badly injured. Two other crewmen were knocked down, but they were not injured. Basil left behind a wife and three small children.

❦

According to the 1900 Census, Miriam's eighty-one-year-old brother, Joseph Cleaves, was living with them. The following year, Miriam received a diagnosis of terminal cirrhosis of the liver. She died that same year at the age of seventy-four and is buried in Caratunk. Her brother, Joseph Cleaves, died the following March of 1902. His cause of death was noted as "working delirium".

Hill's plan involved mortgaging his property to Frank and Alanson Hunnewell, loggers from Bingham and Caratunk. Prior to this commitment, he sold the 1.5 acres on the northeast corner of his property, to Melvin, on May 13, 1903. A condition of this sale required James S. Melvin, his heirs, and assigns to fence and maintain the entire lot.

Shortly thereafter, Melvin, who had been recently logging in Moxie, sold his 1.5-acre homestead to Ethel and Mary Young. Melvin moved to New Vineyard, where he died in 1919.

Slate was found on Lawrence Hill's property in 1905. It was found in the vicinity of Holly Brook. The slate proved to be more lustrous and smoother then the Monson slate and suitable for roofing and mill stock purposes. There were two cost-deterring factors that inhibited the mining of it. First the railroad was six miles away at Mosquito Narrows. Second, the slate was located on a steep slope at Holly Brook. Mining the slate never took place.

Lawrence Hill moved to Norridgewock, and eventually, in 1917, sold his Hangtown farm to Fred Tuttle and Atty. John Holman, both of Athens. Then in 1920, Tuttle and Holman sold it to lumbermen, Alanson and Frank Hunnewell. Later Alanson became sole owner as he foreclosed on Frank in 1946. Hill's lot #26 now belonged to lumberman, Alanson Hunnewell.

Lawrence P. Hill, age sixty-four, died of kidney failure on February 20, 1918 in Emden. He is buried in the Village Cemetery, Caratunk, Maine.

Eventually a part of the Hill's 'Hangtown' homestead became a section of the Appalachian Trail.

Going south of Holly Brook, the homesteaders were referred to as 'the Pleasant Pond Settlement' which included residents of The Forks and Caratunk.

These were Powell's neighbors in the early years. The early homesteaders found hay and potatoes grew well in the rocky soil which also produced an abundance of strawberries, blueberries, and gooseberries. There were currant bushes and apple trees. In the spring, fiddleheads emerged, and at nearby Pleasant Pond fishing was spectacular.

As with all families, everyone was expected to do their share, especially when the men left for logging. After long hours, days, and summer months in the fields, many men turned to logging in the fall, cutting and piling logs. The logs were transported by teams of horses or oxen, harnessed to sleds gliding over the winter snows to nearby streams. Then, they were rafted or surrounded by booms on lakes or stream banks to be dumped into the fast-running waters of spring freshets. The river drivers would then take over, continuing with the log drive.

The children had their chores before and after school. The girls spun wool, wove, made cloth, knitted, washed, cleaned and cooked, dipped candles and more. They also fed chickens, collected eggs, and tended to sheep, goats, and cows. They helped plant gardens, weeded, harvested and preserved foods, including meat and fish. The young boys fed the livestock, lugged firewood, and fetched water from springs and not-so-near wells. They, also, learned how to cook, as many would later become 'cookies' in nearby lumber camps. The older ones cut and split firewood; harvested hay, tilled the rocky fields—where potatoes grew best—and harvested those potatoes. Some learned trades such as blacksmithing, shoeing horses, driving teams, logging, river driving, and hunting, as well as guiding 'sports'—for fishing and hunting—just like their fathers did. The older girls taught reading, writing, and other school subjects to their younger siblings and neighboring children. They taught lessons in homes and in the district's one-room schoolhouse while the teacher held class with the upper grades. There were many school districts as some couples had up to 16 children—and sometimes more. Not all survived, and many did not!

Between 1820 and 1880, a world pandemic occurred with the outbreak of Canker Rash, a form of scarlet fever. It afflicted more children than adults. This airborne and or direct-contact disease caused a rash, fever, sore throat, and ulcerations of the throat and tonsils which led to gangrene and an agonizing death—often within forty-eight hours. Penicillin was not discovered until the 1920s.

The settlers were resourceful and helped each other. They exchanged goods, aided in medical emergencies, and assisted with midwifery. illness, accidents, crop failures, fires, and entertainment that brought neighbors together in both good times and bad.

As McDougall wrote:

It has to do with the people- their resourcefulness–their responsibility–their often rough but fundamental goodness, and their ability to laugh.

—Walter M. McDougall, The Old Somerset Railroad, 2000, Down East Books, Camden, Maine; Pg. 60.

There were barn raisings, shows and fairs at Caratunk featuring draft oxen, logging contests, weekend dances for young and old. They returned home on winter evenings after spirited times of dancing –their favorite being a good polka according to Ida, whose family lived in Moxie Gore.

[Ida Allen's book "ida", The Thorndike Press, 1979]

Riding in a horse-drawn sleigh, partygoers, with heated soap stones under their feet and bundled in homemade quilts, glided home, as their gay laughter preceded their arrival.

The children played games such as Tug of War, Red Rover, Hide and Seek, Tag and Goalie, and Baseball which became popular in the U.S. in the mid-1800s. In the winter, one of the children's favorite games was racing barefoot in the snow, only stopping long enough to warm their feet on heated stones or with large woodchips from the open fire. There was skiing, and sliding on barrel staves and shovels.

At home, board games such as Chess, Checkers and Backgammon were not only played by children but parents would often join in. Some board games were designed to help players learn history, geography, and science. There were also board games to teach the value of working hard and behaving well! Tiddlywinks and Pick-up Sticks helped with coordination. Marbles were a great past time. Regular playing cards and dice were not approved of because they were associated with gambling. Old Maid and Dr. Busby were among the most popular card games. Instead of using dice for a game, one might use a Teetotum which looked like a square wooden top – the flats having numbers, or dots representing numbers. Other entertainment for families was school concerts and plays where the children demonstrated their talents. There were spelling bees, recitals, and singing. Football and baseball games where almost all the settlers would gather to cheer on their teams. "Grownups" would gather to play Whist or Bridge. Enjoyable evenings before the next day's toil.

Everyone lived off the land, woods, water, and 'sports.' Employment for the men evolved around lumbering and trapping in the winter and spring. Spring also brought sport fishermen, who hired guides to show them the nearest honeypot site. The same when fall arrived, and sports came from Massachusetts, New York, Washington, Connecticut, and all over, to bag that big buck, while the homesteaders added income to their always needy family and farms.

It was quite a business catering to the "sports." They provided substantial financial benefits, and, for that matter, they still do today. Many woodsmen turned to guiding, and businesses boomed with the "sports" buying the best rifles, special hunting clothes, and gear to outdo each other. Many came for the experience, some to get their trophy, by whatever means necessary, for bragging rights.

The sports also provided humor, as illustrated in the poem "A Hail to the Hunter" by Holman Day.

A Hail to the Hunter
Oh, we're getting under cover, for the "sport" is on the way.
—pockets bulge with ammunition, and he's coming down to slay:
All his cartridges are loaded and his trigger's on the "half,"
And he'll bore the thing that rustles, from a deer to Jersey calf.

He will shoot the foaming rapids, and he'll shoot the yearling bull.
And the farmer in the bushes—why, he'll fairly get pumped full.
For the gunner is in earnest, he is coming down to kill,
—Shoot you first and then inquire if he hurt you—yes, he will!

For the average city feller he has big game on the brain,
And imagines in October there is nothing else in Maine!
Therefore some absorbed old farmer cutting corn or pulling beans
Gets most mightily astonished with a bullet in his jeans.

So, O neighbor, scoot for cover or get out your armor plate,
—Johnnie's got his little rifle and is swooping on the State.

Oh, we're learning, yes, we're learning,
and I'll warn you now, my Son,
If you really mean to bore us you must bring a bigger gun.

For the farmers have decided they will take no further chance,
And progressive country merchants carry armor-plated pants;
—Carry shirts of chain-plate metal, lines of coats all bullet-proof,
And the helmets they are selling beat a Knight of Malta's "roof."

So I reckon that the farmers can proceed to get their crops,
Yes, and chuckle while the bullet raps their trouser seat and
Stops:
And the hissing double-B shot as they criss-cross over Maine
Will excite no more attention than the patter of the rain.

And the calf will fly a signal and Jersey bull a sign,
And the horse a painted banner, reading "Hoss; Don't Shoot; He's
Mine!"
And every fowl who wanders from the safety of the pen
Will be taught to cackle shrilly, "Please don't plug me; I'm a hen."

Now with all these due precautions we are ready for the gang,
We'll endure the harmless tumult of the rifles crack and bang,
For we're glad to have you with us—shoot the landscape full of
Holes;
We will back our brand-new armor for to save our precious souls.
O you feller in the city, those 'ere woods is full of fun,
We've got on our iron trousers—so come up and bring you gun!

—A Hail to the Hunter by Holman Day, Old
Canada Road Historical Society—Excerpted
from Day, Holman, Up in Maine. Boston: Small,
Maynard & Company, 1900. pp. 162-164.

Take no offense at being called a "sport," we know you are serious hunters or at least most of you are today.

48

Chapter 9

SCHOOL

When Maine was under the laws of Massachusetts (until 1820), for every fifty households in a settlement, one person had to be appointed to teach all children (Common Schools). That person (teacher) was to be paid by parents, masters, or by inhabitants of the area. When there were one hundred families, a high school had to be built and supplied to instruct youths for the University. An average school year was twenty-one weeks plus one day. Sometimes attendance would drop during crop harvesting, and other times due to illness.

In the 1800s, most schools were one room with grades 1-8. The youngest learning their ABCs were known as Abecedarians and the eighth grade was the last class offered in many schools. Sometimes boys and girls were separated in the room.

School supplies mainly consisted of slates and chalk in the early years. Quick learners helped with younger students in the classroom allowing the teacher to focus on giving lessons to upper classmen. Studies included reading, writing, arithmetic, history, grammar, rhetoric, and geography.

There were strict rules for the teachers. They were not allowed to be married or be in a relationship. They could not smoke, drink, or visit where these activities were happening.

Further rules for ladies were: They could not be married and had to be properly dressed without showing their ankles. They were prohibited from having short or dyed hair, attending public dances or pool halls, joining feminist movement groups, and reading the Sunday paper on their day off. They had to be home from 8 p.m. to 6 a.m. and were not allowed to ride with anyone but their father or brother with one exception—they were allowed to be escorted to church by a male other than a relative.

Further rules for men included mandatory attire featuring a necktie or collar. They were prohibited from attending public dances and visiting pool halls.

Besides their teaching duties, both men and women were expected to keep the classroom tidy. They had to lug wood for the stove and make certain the class room was warm prior to the students' daily arrival. They also had to clean the outhouses. Failure to follow these rules was considered grounds for dismissal.

There was strict discipline in the school. School hours were from 9 a.m. to 2 p.m., allowing an hour for lunch (referred to as 'nooning' back then), plus recesses. Later in the 19th century, teachers were required to cook lunch for their students. Eventually, cooks were hired to prepare school lunches.

Prior to World War II, eighty-seven percent of school boards would not hire married women. This practice relaxed after the war, and the percentage dropped to eighteen percent in 1951.

School districts were initiated because of the law that children were not allowed to walk more than a mile to school. Those who lived more than a mile, a teacher would board with the family and the state paid the teacher's salary. Because women were paid less than men, they were more apt to be hired.

In 1847, the average wage for a male teacher was $16.71 a month plus board. Females were paid $6.00 a month exclusive of board. Teaching for more than five years they may see an increase in pay of twenty-five cents, depending on their achievements. It was about this same time that the term "kindergarten" was introduced—Germans in Wisconsin were the first to use this term to describe the earliest grade.

The earliest record I have found involving The Forks Plantation schools is a notice that a meeting was to be held on March 25, 1860 at Ham Shoemakers home to vote for a School Agent. In May of 1861, I found record of three school districts: District 1 with D.P. Williams as agent and 13 scholars; District 2 with W. A. Brown, agent and 19 scholars; and District 3, J.S. Ham, agent with 19 scholars. Also listed was two households Robert Love and C.C. Young who it appears had "live-in teachers" with 6 scholars at Love's home and 9 at Young's.

Teachers lived with the student's families, "boarding around", meaning switching homes every week. In 1892, farm owners were paid 75 cents to $1.50 per week to board teachers. If the accommodations were too "raw" for the teachers they were allowed to take quarters in the hotel.

Students also had to find board and lodging when going out of town for high school.

In 1885, James and Lizzie Powell had four school aged children. At a meeting held at Powell's house, it was decided that the school would be at Justus Adam's house, referred to as the old schoolhouse. The old school house was located on the road into Hangtown before Holly Brook.

There were rotating school agents over the years a few were J. S. Ham, Thomas Morris, Henry Lovejoy, E. G. Morris, and Mark Ham, all farmers and loggers.

In 1893 individual districts were eliminated and town-operated schools came about.

The Washington School (1861-1917) on the Hangtown Road, 1898–1917

The Forks Plantation had three schools: Franklin, Webster, and Washington School. The Washington Schoolhouse was finished in

1894. There was some thought to unite this schoolhouse with the school in Caratunk but it was voted down in 1895.

The Forks, complying with the 1897 State of Maine Law 321 requiring a Superintendent School Committee, voted in C. H. Young, G. S. Bean, and W. S. Powell to be on the committee. Bean was also the truant officer.

It was in 1898, when The Forks Plantation formed a committee of E. G. Morris, G. H. Markham and C. H. Young to "look at the Pleasant Pond School House and to move said house if they see fit to the center of the district." It seems likely that this is when the Washington School was moved to the Hangtown Road.

Image 7. Hangtown school and settler's location, 1905.

This school, an intermediate school with grades four through six, was located on what later became the Hangtown Road, near Holly Brook. At the time it was centralized between Pleasant Pond residents and those north in Hangtown.

The school is shown on the 1905 topographical map. Going from Pleasant Pond north along Hangtown Road, the school was located between the small stream and Holly Brook, on the east side of the road. The dirt foundation can still be located with determination as of 2024. A chimney had been built for this school in 1899, along with a water closet. The budgeted amount was $25.00, and the project to be overseen by James Powell. There is no sign of old bricks on this site to my knowledge. It should be considered that the bricks could have been scavenged for another project. Another possibility is that the chimney was of metal and not brick.

In the early 1900's the Superintendent was instructed to close any school with an average attendance of fewer than eight students, unless he determined otherwise. The attendance at the Washington School did not always meet this requirement and hovered on a decision each year by The Town voters. The Washington school was essential because the children lived too far from the other districts.

The following are some of the teachers at the Washington School (Hangtown):

Nettie Willey of Athens, was a teacher who boarded with Anthony Comber and family at The Forks (Pleasant Pond) when the 1900 census was recorded. She was born in Athens in 1883. Nettie taught from 1899–1903 and was probably the first teacher at the Washington school when Florence Sizeland, her siblings, among others attended the school. When Nettie Willey married in 1903, her teaching career was over.

[In the 1910 census, Nettie, her son Howard D, and her husband Daniel lived in Cornville. He worked as cook at a lumber camp; she at home. By 1920 he was a farmer in Cornville. By 1940 census she was widowed and was a "formsetter" on a farm.]

In 1903 schools were required by law to have twelve school weeks. The Forks Town Meeting in 1904 complied by vote to have twelve weeks in all three districts as according to law. March 21, 1904 was the first record found of The Forks paying tuition for students attending school in other towns.

Kathleen Fox, also a teacher for the Washington School, was paid $82.50 for one session and 97.50 for two sessions. Miss Fox taught in 1906 and 1907, with James Powell serving as agent.

Florence Sizeland lived in Hangtown. She, along with her siblings and neighbors children, attended the Washington school and graduated from there in 1906. Florence taught two sessions at the Washington School in 1907. She attended summer school in Farmington in 1909. Later she not only taught at the Washington School, but was an assistant at the local high school and became a high school teacher in 1910. She went on to attended business college in Portland.

Lila Rowe (Morrison) was also a teacher at the Washington School in 1912 (one-term session earning $46.00); again in 1916 and 17. Lila's teaching career ended when she married Howard Morrison and moved to Vassalboro in 1917. It was law that no married woman was allowed to be a teacher.

[Lila Rowe taught sessions at Pleasant Ridge 1913; Skowhegan 1913; the summer of 1914, she was a bookkeeper for a large farm in Massachusetts and returned to teach at the Albion Healey's district on Pleasant Ridge in 1914. In 1915, she taught sessions at Deadwater, Bingham, and Granville district.]

Velma Sizeland, a younger sister by eight years to Florence was also a teacher. The Forks paid $45.00 for a session in 1916.

Another teacher was Mrs. Iva Pooler. It appears that the town has become more relaxed regarding the rule that women teachers could not be married. Iva Pooler was referred to many times as a Mrs. Pooler. Records show her as a teacher for the Washington School in 1901. Town records have payments to her for sessions in 1915 and 1917. It was in 1917 that the local news reported her having to walk 1½ miles to school through two feet of snow and roads that had not been broken down. Some of the trip she was on snowshoes, making the laborious trip just for four students. This was the last town record that I found of the Washington School. It appears the 'Hangtown' school was closed for good in 1917.

By 1918 every state in the United States had to have a compulsory attendance law in place. Maine's law required that children between the ages of 7 and 17 must attend school unless they already graduated.

Chapter 10

JAMES POWELL REVISITED

THERE WERE NO records indicating that James Powell ever got involved with 'Sport' guiding for it appeared he was way too busy homesteading, logging, and participating in town affairs. However, quite likely he did!

In 1897 he purchased the two hundred acres in Hangtown, from his step-father, William Adams. The Lots 20 and 29, once belonging to Lovejoy.

James gained a new neighbor in 1898 when William Sizeland bought the old Martin farm. There will be more about Sizeland in Chapter 20—the last 100 acres!

James and Lizzie's family continued to grow with twelve children by 1900. Two children had died, James E. in the 1870s, and Mary Elizabeth in 1890. Still at home were William H., eighteen; Agnes A., sixteen; Alfred A., twelve; Winfield S., six; and twins Alta M. and Avis E. age four. Powell's farm was mortgaged as many landowners did when they needed to borrow money to sustain themselves – there were no banks around back then. Their homesteads became collateral for loans to hold them by until the next harvest. Sometimes they promised their harvest as collateral perhaps to buy that badly needed work horse or just for necessary cash. The work horse may even become collateral. In 1906, James sold his west lot #20 to William Forsyth and Edward W. Heath, leaving James with 100 acres. By 1910, he had also purchased 5 acres of lot #30, with buildings, from Alanson Hunnewell, which seems to have been where his first home was before moving onto the old Lovejoy homestead.

Lizzie, Powell's wife of forty-nine years, died of acute hepatitis on April 8, 1919, at the age of sixty-five. She was predeceased by three of her children. Two previously mentioned, and the third, Agnes A., was twenty-one when she died in 1905. Powell was still living and farming in Hangtown with sons, Alfred, thirty-two and Winfield twenty-seven. When the census was taken, his sons were working at a lumber camp. Over the years, Powell's farm and properties were constantly mortgaged—more land bought—and land sold. In 1925, he sold the remainder of his holdings, including land, his home and buildings to a well-known logger, Alanson Hunnewell. He then moved nearer to the Kennebec River, The Forks Plantation.

Powell had been very much involved with The Forks Plantation town affairs over the years. He filled positions such as Truant Officer, Accessor, Tax Collector, and he was on the Board of Health which was first organized in 1898. James E. Powell Jr, a much respected citizen died at The Forks on June 11, 1929, at the age of 79. He is buried at The Forks Bean Cemetery on the Mountain Road.

Chapter 11

WHO IS HUNNEWELL?

IT IS TIME to introduce Alanson Gammon Hunnewell, who becomes quite a player in the forward history of Hangtown.

Hunnewell was originally from Moscow, born February 1874 to Edward J. and Sarah L. Hunnewell. His brothers were Charles, Frank, Fred, Jordan, & Manly. He attended school through the eighth grade. Like many young men growing up, he became a lumberman first working as a laborer. By the age of twenty-six, he worked as a river driver.

Somewhere between 1900 and 1910, he moved from Moscow to Caratunk, where he lodged with Ora and Annie (Webster) Savage. He was a timber surveyor. In 1907, he began logging in Hangtown, after purchasing the Powell lot (#30) from Herbert Prince.

In 1920, Hunnewell was single and farming on his own land in Caratunk. He was still in the lumbering business and obtained additional property in Hangtown. He acquired the homesteads of Lawrence Hill and Ethel Young from Fred Tuttle. Hunnewell went on to purchase the James Powell homestead #29 in 1925. He continued this livelihood into the 1930s. By the 1940 census, he was, once again, a lodger at the Savage House. Ora Savage had passed away, and Annie was the head of household. Annie's sister, Eva Webster aged fifty-six, was also listed as a lodger. Hunnewell reported working seventy hours a week on a non-profitable farm, although he noted that he had additional sources of income.

Hunnewell's home, as described in 1950, was a farm located about one mile from the village on the right. At seventy-six, he was the head of the household and never married. Hunnewell described himself as a country squire, the owner of a lumber business and an estate manager. Eva Webster was listed as his maid, and employed in a private home.

In 1958, Hunnewell acquired more land. William F. Hunnewell, willed the Spaulding Farm, located near the river, to Alanson G. Hunnewell and Eva L. Webster as joint tenants, and not tenants in common.

Alanson Hunnewell served a total of seventeen years as a Caratunk selectman. He passed away on May 24, 1961 leaving everything, including the land in Hangtown, to Eva Webster. He is buried in the Village Cemetery in Bingham.

Eva L. Webster was born February 24, 1884, in Caratunk to Edward and Abby (Clark) Webster. Eva was one of ten children.

In the 1910 census, Eva was twenty-four and single. She and her sixty-six-year-old widowed mother, Abby, were living in Waterville with Eva's cousin, Florence B. Gifford. By 1930, Eva had relocated to Caratunk, where she worked for her sister and brother-in-law, Annie and Ora Savage, at their boarding house.

Eva and her sister, added a 'tea room' to the boarding house in 1920. Their pleasant rooms attracted travelers from near and far. Eva continued to live and work with Annie, who in 1940, was seventy-four and widowed.

Eva Webster never married. She was the first female tax collector for Caratunk, holding that office for eight years. She was very involved with town affairs, a member of The Woman's Club, and active in school projects, such as the forming of the Red Schoolhouse Association. Eva advertised in the local papers, selling items such as threads, bobbins and shuttles. She offered bronze turkey eggs for hatching at twenty-five cents each, and the bronze turkeys could be purchased by the pair or single!

[Bronze turkeys have become quite rare nowadays,
as the industry prefers the faster-growing breeds.]

After a brief illness, Eva passed away at the Augusta hospital on May 21, 1968, at the age eighty-four. Eva L. Webster was laid to rest in the Village Cemetery in Caratunk.

Both, Alanson Hunnewell's and Eva Webster's, names will surface later in Hangtown's history.

Chapter 12

ORIGINS OF HANGTOWN ROAD

LIFE WAS NOT easy living out of town on those homesteads in the late 1800s. There were no roads just horse and oxen trails. The trails were rough and bumpy with roots and rocks, wheel ruts, and a path in the middle stomped out by the horse's hooves. The farmers and loggers had difficulties transporting their families, products, and supplies.

Their children traveled these rough roads, often through deep snow, and blustery, freezing, stormy weather to get to the one-room school house. Spring brought rain and mud for both students and their teacher to trudge through in their galoshes- if they were so lucky to have a pair- as they made their way along the old horse path. Women finding themselves alone, needing medical help, worried about the doctor's delayed arrival- perhaps giving birth before he arrived. There were times when he was too late to save a life- or two.

Wanting better traveling conditions, in 1879 partitions were being executed for a road leading from the Pleasant Pond road north to Powell's—eventually to continue through to The Forks Village and intersect with the River Road—later called route 201 or Old Canada Road.

On August 4, 1879, Lawrence Hill, as was discussed earlier, owned the farm and land immediately north and south of the Holly Brook Bridge. He presented a petition to the Somerset County Commissioners for the construction of a county road that would extend to his farm. He and seven others proposed the road to begin—

. . . at some point on the Pleasant Pond Road, so called, in Caratunk Plantation, and leading thence in the most direct and practicable route, to some point near the house of Lawrence P. Hill in the Forks Plantation.

—Daily Kennebec journal, August 14, 1879; Chronicling America. com; Digitized Newspapers.

This road was started late in 1879. Beginning at Barrett's Spaulding's house (Caratunk side of the Pleasant Pond Road), it passed by Albert's Spaulding's house (The Forks Plantation), continued to Justus Adams north field and on to Hill's farm, where it ended.

The next year and a series of years afterwards, Hill's northern neighbors, Martin, Lovejoy, Devoll, and Powell, proceeded with petitions for a continuance of this road past their farms. Ultimately intersecting with the existing county road—route 201—then known as the River Road— near the Forks Village.

[Petitions: Daily Kennebec journal, September 23, 1880 signed by David Devoll and 19 others; Daily Kennebec journal, September 06, 1881, Image 4 signed by Barrett Spaulding, & 43 others; The Somerset Reporter, August 09, 1900, Page 8 partition of James S. Melvin.]

In 1882, the order from the County Commissioners of Summerset County on the petition follows:

It is Ordered, that there be assessed on the following described township in said county of Somerset, the sum set against said township, for the purpose of making and opening a County road as laid out by the County Commissioners of said County of Somerset of Lawrence P. Hill and others in 1879, in The Forks Plantation.

—Daily Kennebec Journal, January 14, 1882 Image 2

The seven residents, each owning roughly 100 acres, paid a tax to of $10.00 each—totaling $70.00. Let it also be noted that owners of vast tracts of timberland such as Coburn, Clark, American Realty Company which was branch of International Paper Company, Umbagog, and others, contributed to the tax, as well.

This tax continued through the years and was collected for the County. The County Commissioner usually appointed one of the property owners along this road to collect this tax, e.g. Lawrence Hill in 1879, David Devoll in 1880, Barrett Spaulding 1881, Hill again in 1882, 1888 by James Martin, 1890 by Barrett Spaulding, 1899 by James Powell, and so forth. In the early days this road was called the Pleasant Pond Road to The Forks, and later it became known as the Hangtown Road.

[In 1893, Congress authorized Rural Free Delivery— only if the road was gravel or macadam.]

This and other roads were a lifeline to all. When snow made them impassable, farmers, workers, and loggers gathered in groups to shovel them. As an example, recorded in 1898, Joseph Spaulding's crew needing provisions, was given the task of shoveling a road for eight miles from the Spaulding Logging Camp to Dan Patience's The West Forks Hotel. Another crew was shoveling the road from there to Parlin Pond which was roughly ten miles. At the same time, Anthony Comber and crew shoveled four miles in order to get supplies to the workers and their teams. The storm had started at noon on Sunday with snow and continued through Tuesday with hail—snow again on Wednesday, rain on Thursday forenoon and snow and rain at intervals on Friday and Saturday. The storm left nearly four feet of snow, as reported in the Somerset Reporter on March 03, 1898.

Not everyone was accommodated with the new county road. Melvin petitioned in 1900 for a connecting road from his house to the Pleasant Pond to The Forks Road (later the Hangtown Road). His house was located about one-quarter of a mile east of the existing road. The hearing was held at Sizeland's (Martin's old place) and was later denied by The Commissioner. Melvin then requested the town to construct the road. However, I found no further record of Melvin's request.

[Many years later, Boise Cascade built the Crossover road—a road connecting the Boise Road to the Hangtown road and it is still in existence today. This road passed very close to where Melvin's house was once located.]

A deed dated 1903, shows the name Hangtown Road was already in use. In the Town Clerk's report of March 18, 1907, it was voted that James Powell be Road Commissioner for the roads lying in the southeast corner of The Forks Plantation, known as the Pleasant Pond District. The Hangtown Road was one of these roads. Later, on February 1, 1919, The Daily Kennebec's local news reported that Mark Merrill and Carroll Hunnewell were hauling cedar from Hangtown to the mill.

To the best of my knowledge most of the land owners along the Hangtown Road were farmers. Some owned their farms, some were mortgaged. Many also logged for themselves or for logging outfits. The men were busy winters - guiding, trapping and or logging. Working in the woods was the only source of income for many men. They spent fourteen to eighteen hours a day logging. While working in the woods -leaving their families to work the farm - they stayed in remote lumber camps. Bunk beds lined the walls, with a sack filled with evergreen boughs, hay or straw serving as a mattress. Fifteen to twenty men might sleep head-to-toe, all sharing one enormous blanket. There were cooks, as well as cook's helpers who were known as cookies. Some camps had fire pits in the center for cooking and heating. Outside, pits with burning coals sported iron pots filled with beans, which were set amongst the coals and covered with earth for the night. By morning the beans would be ready for breakfast and the other meals. Cooks used cross poles over the fires to suspend pots of tea or simmering food. They used reflectors for baking things like pies and biscuits.

Winters made it easy for the woodsman to move the logs from the woods to the streams. The ice and snow allowed the loaded sleds to glide more easily as they were hauled out by teams of horses or oxen to the banks of the rivers and estuaries. In the spring, the men rolled and pushed them into the flood waters. There the river-drivers drove the floating logs downstream to join with other company's logs and continue on to the trains or mills. Men positioned themselves in strategic locations along the river where they waited in case there was a log jam. Some loitered long enough to find gold.

Chapter 13

FINDING GOLD

BACK IN THE spring of 1891, one of the Kennedy boys and Scott Durgin, who were river men, discovered gold. Most believed this discovery would likely have been on the Enchanted or a tributary stream. It is assumed they found it when they were in that area for a log drive. Many surmised the mine to be high in the timber region but no one seemed to know exactly where, as the boys kept that a secret. They hiked to the woods every spring and worked the mine, panning gold. No big chunks were found, yet they washed out enough gold to make four dollars a day all summer. It appears they made good money for they bought some of the best lands along the Kennebec farming region. Old hunters and guides tried to track the boys, to no avail. A Skowhegan jeweler handled their gold.

[Several jewelers were active locally around 1890–1891 included W. C. Pearson, George Philbrick of Water Street, and Baxter of Temple Street.]

Their gold mine still seems to be a secret today. Perhaps for the same reason as the story that The Somerset Reporter published on July 21, 1898, pg3.

Nugget's Luck

How the spruce looking stranger got into the little old, dilapidated town up in the Sierras none of its inhabitants appeared to know, but most of them were extremely anxious to ascertain. Seldom it was that any one went to the town. Apparently there was no particular reason why any one should. The surrounding scenery was grand, it is true, but the town could make no claim to being an essential part of the grandeur. Its one street straggled up the mountainside for a short distance and lost its way in the forest. A long, ramshackle "hotel," several despondent looking stores and a number of saloons made up what it was pleased to call the business portion of the town. On all sides and as far as the eye could see, however, were the imperishable evidences of what this little town once had been – the center of a natural wealth almost inconceivable. Vast areas of white and yellow and reddish clay, mountains seamed and gashed and cut in twain, miles of rusty and disjointed gigantic iron pipes, told of the days when the miners with hydraulic guns "held up" nature and forced it to deliver its treasure.

But all that was long ago and is only a pleasant memory with the little town now, and to the stranger's not unnatural inquiry as to how the people supported themselves came the cheerful and cannibalistic reply that they "lived on one another."

The stranger sat on a box outside one of the stores beside one of the citizens and soon found himself listening to a monologue offered for his entertainment. It would have been a dialogue between them, but the entertainer would not have it that way. An old man, with grizzled beard and weather beaten face, was he. The stranger noticed with some surprise, that, although stained and rusty, his long frock coat and the trousers stuck into his boots were of good broadcloth. A very conspicuous watch chain, a huge diamond pin in a setting of tobacco stained shirt front and the entire absence of a collar made up a somewhat incongruous appearance.

"Yes, you're right," began the entertainer, starting the monologue with considerable energy, "this town ain't worth a whoop in hell today, but you oughter seen it onct. Ain't a forty-niner myself, and you got to make a good deal of allowance for what some o' these old has been tell you, but they all do say it was a hummer before they stopped hydrauleekin.

"You oughter get old Nuggets to tell you somethin about it. Ain't you met Nuggets yet? Well, you should, for he's about the only sight we got in town —only thing the town brags about and p'ints out to strangers. Nuggets was here- or som'ers about here- before they ever did any hydrauleeking- when everything was placer and sluice minin. He'll tell you his story. He'll tell it without bein ast. I've heard it so often that I know it myself. He likes to hear himself talk.

"He was one o' the first to come acrost the plains-leastways that' what he says-and when got here he just nacherally staid. He kem around by the old emigrant trail back o' Lake Tahoe and into Hangtown.

"Hangtown-you know, that's what they called Placerville in them days-was a great place then. Meals was $3, and so was beds; whisky was four bits and two bits a drink, accordin as how you wanted it, and flour was $10 for a small sack. Course, you know, most all supplies kem around the Horn to Frisco, was boated up to Sacramento and teamed out to the mines from there.

"Business was good in California in them days. Most every one had money, and it wasn't no trick to get it. The cricks and river bottoms was full o' gold, and any one could take a shovel, pick and rocker and wash out as much as he liked. Course that sort o' thing spoilt the Argonauts, as they call 'em, or good many of 'em anyhow -would a-spoilt most any one.

Kinder seemed to them that the supply would last forever, and they didn't worry much and wasn't particular about savin it. They was all about alike, and after a fellow had worked purty hard for awhile and cleaned up a little pile he'd get to thinkin he needed relaxation, and down he'd go to Frisco and blow in his pile.

"Then he'd strike the trail for the goldfields for another stack o' blue chips.

"Course every one had a partner in them days, and this here Nuggets had one by name o' Wilkins. One day they kem into this town with a nugget that was a corker. Was as big as your hat -red cinnabar, with chunks of pure gold stickin out of it all around.

"The Jeweler offered 'em $1500 for it, but they wouldn't sell it. Nuggets said there was more o' it where it kem from, but no one believed him.

"Everybody thought that Nuggets and Wilkins had found a small pocket, and that was all there was to it, but some o' these pockets are good enough for a pore man anyhow.

"That night there was an awful windstorm, and two days afterward Nuggets was found comin out o' Rattlesnake canyon over there plum crazy.

They brought him into town, and all they could get out o' him was a string o' the d—dest, foolishest words you ever heard of. He didn't say much else for a good many years afterward- youster sit around the town here and get it off to himself. Went something like this:

"Changed all the trees in the Rattlesnake-moved 'em and mixed 'em all up. Might 'a' been a dream, but I don't think so. Ask Bill -he knows. Put a shot in her. Seen rock in my time, but no rock like that. Bill, d——d old fool, gets scared, and we kivered her up to come back to. Didn't blaze no tree, but left my old knife's stickin on the moss side o' that tree. Might 'a' been a dream. Ask bill.'

"Course you can bet your life that old canyon was prospected pretty well after that, but nothing was found. The specimen was sold and the money divided between Bill Wilkins and Nuggets' daughter, who had to take care o' him. Wilkins went over in Calaveras soon after that and fell down a shaft about 500 feet deep.

"Well, time went by, and the law stopped hydrauleeking, and purty much every one left the town that could git out o' it, and it ain't been worth a d—n sence.

"Nuggets' daughter she married Bob Hittel, who was a teamster and didn't have much o' it to do either. They was pore, but they managed to make a livin and keep old Nuggets besides. Course you know the old man couldn't do nothing but sit around and talk those words I told you of.

"Every one was kind to him, except, perhaps, Jake Openheimer, who kept the principal store then. He youster rile him a good deal and josh him and ask him when he was goin to open her up, but I reckon he didn't mean a great deal o' harm.

"Every now and then Nuggets 'ud wander over into Rattlesnake canyon and spend nigh on to a day there. When he'd come back, he'd be worse tuk than ever and go moonin around and saying those words: 'Changed all the trees in the Rattlesnake- moved 'em and mixed 'em all up. Might a-been a dream, but I don't think so.'

" 'Bout this time his little gran'son was growing up, and Nuggets began for to take him along with him in his trips to the canyon. Mrs. Hittel, she objected at first, but when she seen the boy liked to go and her father was dead set on havin him with him she didn't make no more objections. The boy used to say that while they was in the canyon Nuggets spent most o' his time huntin for something he couldn't find.

"One evenin in the summer time, 'bout ten years ago-I was here then myself-Nuggets and the boy kem into town and gave it a surprise that it ain't got over sence. You can believe it or not as you want to, but he'd got back his mind all right and talked as sensibly as I'm talking now. Don't believe he ever was crazy myself -just think he'd got his mind set on one thing and couldn't get it off.

"But he was purty near crazy with happiness. He'd an old rusty knife in his had and he kept sayin to us all the time, ' 'Twarn't no dream after all, 'twarn't no dream.' Seems when they was in the canyon the boy got to playin around and crawled under a big tree that 'ad been blown down and found the knife stickin in it underneath. Course you know what that meant.

"Well. Nuggets is all right now. So was his claim. He sold it for a purty nice sum to a couple o' big mining men down below. See those smokestacks in the trees over in the canyon? Well, there's a 14 stamp mill on the spot where that knife was found.

"Bob Hittel runs this store we're a-sittin in front of, and Bob's wife owns her own house. Nuggets has a mortgage on about everything Jake Openheimer's got left, and the boy - the gran'son, you know -he's down below in business for himself."

"That's about the story old Nuggets 'll tell you when you meet him. Some o' it's true I know myself for a fact, and I reckon, mebbe, some o' it's –well, you know, Nuggets is a Missourian and a purty good liar himself."

The stranger arose, stretched himself, and, striding up the street, encountered the one legged druggist standing in the doorway of his store.

"Great story I just heard," said the stranger.

"Been talking to the old pioneer?"

"Pioneer? Why he's not a forty-niner."

"No, but he's a forty-eighter."

"Who is he, anyhow?"

"Him? Oh, that's Nuggets."

—William A. Taaffee in Argonaut (Author)

Yet, a more local story can be found in the November 03, 1898 issue of The Somerset Reporter on page 6. This story, or perhaps yarn, took place in 1858 in The Forks, Maine, and was written by a New York Sun correspondent.

Forty Years Ago

A New York Sun correspondent appears to be responsible for the following yarn and locates it at The Forks, Maine:

More than 40 years ago old Jim Dolliver, a rich owner of timber land and mills buried $42,000 in gold somewhere between here and Murphy's.

[This was Nicholas W. Murphy, owner in 1885
of the Old Boise Hotel on the West side
of the Canada Road at Parlin Pond.]

He had come from Montreal along the old French voyageur's trail, and, reaching The Forks, had told the landlord of the hotel that he had been followed by a party of French and Indian out-laws all the way from the St. Lawrence river.

"I have nearly five score hundred yellow sovereigns in my batteau," said he, "and if I don't bury my money now the crazy devils will rob me before I get to Waterville."

He left the hotel at 10 o'clock that night, and was away three days. On his return he remarked to the landlord:

"Well, I've put that money where the arch-angel Gabriel can't find it."

Then he took a hearty supper, went to bed, slept two days and two nights, and awoke a raving maniac. For a week he fought Indians and buried untold treasures in his delirum, and died in the act of shooting a Mohawk chief, who had invaded his sick fancy for the purpose of robbing him. Papers found among his effects showed that he had drawn Lb.,500 in English gold from a Montreal bank a month before he arrived at The Forks and as this sum did not appear inventory of his estate, it was believed generally that the money was buried within a day's journey of this post office.

For a dozen years after Dolliver's death his heirs advertised for the missing wealth and increased the reward until the finder was entitled to 75 percent of all he should discover. Having spent nearly $3,000 in advertising, the heirs gave it up as a bad job, after which the people who knew the story continued the work at their own expense. For 20 years the digging went on at all season. Whenever a man or boy ran short of money and had nothing else to do he shouldered a pick and shovel and, taking a week's supply of food on his back, went into the woods between Murphy's and The Forks and went to digging. Some located the treasure in dreams, others made deep excavations in mellow hillsides where the labors were light, and very many hired expert diviners with apple limbs and witch hazel rods to help them along on the road to wealth.

In October, 1880, Saunders Atwood came here from Winterport and brought an electric battery with him, which he said could detect an English farthing under four "fathoms" of solid earth. When he went away two weeks later he showed a handful of English sovereigns all stamped with dates 30 or more years ago, and said that he had unearthed the whole of the missing wealth. But while the people accepted his theory that the proper time to dig was on the dark of an October moon, they repudiated the story that he had found any of the missing coin. This fall when the muscles of the farmers had grown hard from digging potatoes, about 40 men packed up a few tools and made ready to start on another search for Dolliver's money as soon as the old moon should change. They were loafing about the hotel and store one night when word came from Montreal that Eugene Beaupre, and aged and rich Frenchman of that city, had lately died, confessing on his deathbed that he had seen Dolliver conceal the gold in a hollow pine stub and had gone and taken it away after the rightful owner had returned to The Forks. This information was verified later by an announcement that one Eugene Beaupre, late of Montreal, had died and left an estate amounting to $60,000 to different charities, in Canada and Maine, saying in his will that the gift was made as a "partial atonement for a grievous sin committed in the State of Maine in October, 1856.

Conservative estimates indicate that more than 12,000 days of hard labor have been expended in digging for Dolliver's wealth, and that fully 30,000 tons of earth and stone have been dug up and turned over by men who were looking in Maine for money that was safely invested in Montreal real estate.

—The Somerset reporter, [volume], November 03, 1898, Page 6,

Image 6. Chronicling America: Historic American Newspapers. Lib. Of Congress

I can imagine farmers reading these articles as the entire family sits around the kitchen woodstove enthralled with the concept of finding gold on or near their property. Alike minds rush across the fields, inspecting rocks and checking every crevice until fatigued and retrieving what is real. As the candle's flickering flame of light dwindles, so do their visions of wealth. The woodstove is stoked for the night and the reality is that their chores will be there in the morn.

Chapter 14

FISTICUFFS AND MORE

River Drivers vs Immigrants 1885

THERE WAS QUITE a rivalry, often times fueled by alcohol, between the River Drivers and the Frenchmen. Frenchmen often migrated to The Forks area to work in the farmer's hay fields and later to pick bushels, upon bushels, of potatoes during harvest time. Of course the River Drivers were mostly men from nearby towns. When not river-driving these men were farmers, woodsmen, guides for the sportsmen, cooks for lumber camps, or whatever work they could find to further support their families. The men were often accompanied by their sons who learned the trade in their early years including how to defend themselves during a confrontation. As with Azel Adams, when he punched a classmate for copying his work, the teacher grabbed Azel by his collar and necktie, leaving a mark on his neck. Azel's father insisted that he handle it himself and go back to give the teacher a licking—which Azel did!

[Taken from Creative Survival: A Narrative History of Azel Adams, The Forks, Maine, compiled by Sally K. Butcher.]

Sometimes a little disturbance, often with the migrating Frenchmen, developed into fisticuffs.

The Forks Riot

There seemed to be quite a fight recorded back in July of 1885. So much so, for days it made the newspapers from Skowhegan–to Aroostook County–to Portland! The Forks Riot, a fierce fight, as reported, was between River-drivers and Frenchmen. A number of Canadian Frenchmen, with their teams, were on their way to obtain work at the hayfields- some delivering freight. Freighted with produce, liquor, and tobacco, they were abruptly stopped by thirteen river-drivers who robbed them and tipped over their wagons as they passed by the river, near The Forks. The Frenchmen retaliated by fighting and it was reported that one fired his weapon five times, twice hitting one man whom they believed would succumb to his wounds. This was answered with a shotgun blast from the river-drivers and it seems one of these attackers was hit on the head with an axe. It was once reported that this man was killed. Further investigation proved he was not. As a matter of fact, he was found to not have been in the fight at all, but away up river with his girlfriend! The fight went on from 2 o'clock in the afternoon until 10 that evening, with all but one of those in the fight still standing.

Over fifty men were stopped, 100 bushels of oats, 30 gallons of liquor, and a quantity of tobacco was obtained by the highway men. The River Drivers were all arrested with the exception of one who escaped as reported by the Daily Kennebec Journal's July 11, 1885 issue.

Another news article had a slightly different version. It seems that it was a party of four Frenchmen who were stopped, and demanded of their money and whiskey. Three of the Frenchmen ran, while the fourth slashed into the assailants, sinking the blade into the back of one, cropping an arm off another, and splitting the head of a local, 'notorious troublemaker'—who was reported to be senseless.

There were further reports all the way from Aroostook County that one of the drivers passed-by five days after the fight, being supported by two men. His face and body were beaten to a pulp. Another man was said to have been nearly beaten to death, thrown twenty feet over the bank and into the Kennebec.

As The Portland Daily Press related in their July 16, 1885 article The Fight at The Forks, there seemed to be several fights that day of the Fourth. It was reported by the railroad driver that the River Drivers stopped a Canadian team, and knocked over the wagon. After consuming what whiskey they stole, they stationed themselves by the road, continued their thievery and drunkenness while picking more fights.

Portland Daily's article ends with assuring all travelers, that the road to The Forks is safe traveling, day or night, and that any attempt to magnify such affairs into tragedies, is ridiculous.

Then There Was the Forks Battle

A Frenchmen was passing by a locals home when the old man of the house started throwing stones at him. The Frenchmen promptly retaliated by returning the stones. The man's son came from the house to aid in his father's plight. The old man, exasperated called for his wife to bring the shotgun. His son took the gun from his mother and shot the Frenchmen who then ran away. Later it was found that he had non-life threatening hits- one in the back and one under the arm. The assailants tried to make the Frenchmen the aggressor and under the influence of liquor. Having no proof of this, they, themselves, were placed under $500 bond for appearance at the next court.

There is quite evidently a bitter feeling between the Frenchmen and drivers in The Forks region and it would not be strange if there was more fighting.

—Daily Kennebec Journal, July 15, 1885

Ah, But Apples Do Not Fall Far From the Tree—Do They

Five years later we find members of the same family as assailants on a traveler who was attacked by their dog. The traveler, trying to walk away, grabbed a stake from the home's ground to ward off the dog. The owner insisted he put the stake back but the man refused unless the dog was called off. Upon continuing to walk away, the owner's son followed the man about 40 rods, then knocked him down and beat him. The case was tried at Bingham and the dog owner was fined $10.00 and costs. He appealed to the December term of court in Skowhegan. The outcome is unknown by me.

A little discussion between Henry Lovejoy and Ruel Churchill on the Pleasant Pond Road ended in Lovejoy getting hurt. Churchill was hauled away to Norridgewock by Sheriff Charles Brown. However, on the way, Churchill jumped from the wagon and escaped . . . October 1890.

Sometimes people were wrongly accused as reported in the Kennebec Journal, January 03, 1895:

"Caratunk and The Forks have been having quite a scare of late, by what was pronounced tramp. Gardens have been robbed, cows have been milked, houses broken into, cellars have been robbed of their contents—fruit, cake and pie. Stores have been broken into, men's clothing and money taken by supposed tramps." Fighting for the truth, it was discovered that a couple of townsmen were guilty of the stealing.

Not all fights were of this kind. There was the fight against illnesses such as smallpox in 1885, in which many died. Whole families—children of all ages—mothers ill and leaving their husband to care for all the children—husbands ill, or dying and leaving their wives and children to fend for themselves. Settlers were very leery of the immigrants, watching them carefully, avoiding contact, for they often brought illnesses such as typhoid to the homesteaders.

Life went on, battling against drought, snow storms, lightning strikes and fires. Oh yes, including the very long battle to get a road to Hangtown.

Chapter 15

HANGTOWN GETS
ITS NAME

So, just how did Hangtown get its name? Let me just say that I have found a question can be answered, modified and expounded on, believed and not believed, and made more believable or not so believable! As to the following answers I got from asking this question to multiple people I will let you judge the answer – or perhaps you know the real answer?

My sources are confidential unless otherwise noted since I do not want to take chances on the possibility of adding a more current 'Hangtown' news story!

First, let me start with a true Hangtown story which does not take place in The Forks, Somerset County, nor even in Maine. It will support my previous statement.

It takes place in what is now known as Placerville, California in 1849. The story goes, that there were five immigrants who attempted to rob a Mexican gambler. They were caught, but never got to trial since a mob hanged them on a large oak tree-right on Main Street. There is, of course, some discrepancy as to the total five being hanged—some say just three Frenchmen and one Chilean, who were known to be wanted men.

Others say there was a trial and a question asked, "What shall be done with them?"—The majority won with, "Hang them." Regardless of the correct story, because of the multiple hangings, a Californian history professor insists only four were hanged, while a museum and curator claims twenty-one or twenty-two. The name Hangtown was given to this small town which was previously known as Dry Diggings—referring to the way miners had to remove the soil and relocate it to water for washing out the gold.

Of course, there are other versions of the story. This version, according to the local museum there, states that three outlaws were hanged for shooting their guns as they rode through town. The end result seems to be the same.

Ah, wait now—another version of the California story from a similar article states that three men were hanged for cattle rustling, according to https://westernmininghistory.com. In 1849, three men were convicted and hanged for robbing a miner in his hotel room. Then there were the three men who were hanged for robbing a success-ful prospector—probably the same story! I wonder how many other stories appeared in local newspapers—or how many men actually were hanged in 'Hangtown!'

Between the Temperance league and local churches the name Hangtown, California, was changed to Placerville in 1854. Placerville still exploits their old name with local shop signs, the site of the hang-man's platform, and the legendary 'Hangtown Fry,'—a dish including eggs, bacon, and oysters. Maybe the most controversial item was a mannequin named George, raised by a noose, which hung above the Old Hangman's Tree (now the local ice cream parlor). An attempt was made to clean up Placerville with the removal of the dummy, but public opinion insisted on George's return. Ah, but the dummy was stolen in 2015—for what reason? A subject for more local gossip!

No gossip in this—it was unanimously voted to remove the hangman's noose from Placerville's city logo in April 2021—the name, 'Hangtown.' remained!

Ahh, remember, "History is a fiction created by those who survive." ~ Linda Tatelbaum, Carrying Water–A Way of life, About Time Press, Appleton, Maine.

Welcome to Hangtown, Maine

When I bought a camp in Hangtown, The Forks Plantation, Maine in 2006, as fitting to the roads name, an old noose could still be found hanging in one of the Balm of Gilead trees.

[A cross between the poplar and cottonwood trees. They have large trunks and can grow 75–100 feet tall and the canopy can be 40 feet wide. Dark-green oval leaves with pointed tips—the underside whitish-green with orange veins, and native to North America, Eastern U.S. zones. Some have been found to be 100 years old. The buds have a turpentine aroma and were collected to make herbal medicines and fragrances—sometimes used for embalming purposes.]

The noose, attached to one of the tree-sized limbs of the Balm of Gilead, worn and weathered, dangled before my raised eyes, causing my researching mind to wonder about the stories it harbored. Since it could not tell me the stories perhaps neighbors or old timers could. I became obsessed with the idea or finding out the story or yarn behind the name of Hangtown and the noose!

Thinking the quickest way to find out, I asked the previous property owner.

"I'm not sure where it came from . . . it was so high up I didn't notice it until someone pointed it out one morning," as he hurried about his business not wanting to say more.

That was very little help, I thought. I decided to ask anyone who walked by if they knew any history of the area.

Early one morning, as I walked the old Hangtown Road, I met another camp owner. After the introductions, I didn't hesitate to ask about his knowledge of the noose and Hangtown.

With a shrug of the shoulders his answer was: "Not really sure, been wund'ring myself . . . didn't notice it at first and no one else around knew neither. One thing was said tho'- believed a young man got into some trouble messin 'round with farmer's dawter. He was known to git into trouble enough—that young man—and back then weren't northing for public to take care of things themselves."

That raised my eyebrows! Determined to dig deeper, I approached other locals, only to hear different versions of what seemed like the same story.

"A young man known for committing crimes raped a young girl and the public back then took care of their own. He was promptly hanged at Hangtown," I was told.

Another offered this:

"I was told that a school teacher back a ways was hung in that tree there," as he pointed to the Balm in Gilead tree where the noose still hung about twenty-five feet off the ground. He added, "I never found out the reason from the tight-lipped homesteader and wondered if an angry, protective mother found out her favorite had his ears boxed by the teacher and insisted her husband teach the teacher!!! Perhaps things went just a little too far!!" He tipped his orange hat, he smiled and walked on with, "Nice day isn't it?"

My mind went into overdrive, recalling the old news articles I had recently read—the hotel owner who left town, and the shepherd found down river. Could Moses Burnham and his accomplice, if they indeed committed the crime, have hanged the Irish shepherd, Mitchel Berry, in Hangtown, and then disposed of his body in the river? Had the neighbors suspected this? The record shows that Berry's body was found at the river near the Atwood farm in Bingham and the autopsy revealed that he had no water in his lungs.

[Source: The Forks of the Kennebec, Marilyn Sterling-Gondek, Old Canada Road Historical Society, page 189.]

Could things have gotten so out of hand between the River Drivers and Frenchmen? Oh, and what about the tramps? Encouraged by news reporting, the locals became very wary of the tramps.

"There has been a swarm of tramps this way for the last two weeks, all looking for work and hoping to find none," writes the Daily Kennebec Journal, May 1898.

The settlers were not just leery of them but disgusted with them as well. Maybe the tramps, who would not move on, just disappeared. No one would miss them. Like the ones who stopped at a number of farms asking for oats, meal, pork, and potatoes. After receiving the goods, they promised to return the next day with baskets for payment but were never seen again as written in the Samoset Reporter, May 19, 1898.

Was there so much suspicion of hangings in this area of the Balm of Gileads that Hangtown was born? Maybe!

In the late afternoon, as my friend and I were riding on the Hangtown Road, we encountered an older, balding, white-haired gentleman batting blackflies as he walked towards his parked pickup. It was a bit unusual to see someone parked at the crossroads, so we pulled in beside his black Toyota to say hello—obviously a bit curious as to what he was doing so far back in the woods.

As we said our hellos, he offered that he had just finished a short, yearly hike on the Appalachian Trail.

[This part of the Trail is located crossing the Hangtown Road on the north end of Holly Brook Bridge.]

He was such a curious looking man. He seemed too old to be hiking, carrying a walking stick, yet he appeared so agile. Smiling readily, ducking, and swatting at flies swarming around his sweaty head, he turned towards our jeep.

"Oh, I come up here every once in a while," he continued, "use ta drive down this road all the way to The Forks. But since the homesteaders left, the road got growd up with no use."

"Are you from Caratunk then?" I asked, as I leaned sideways to talk out the driver's side window.

"What's that," he asked as he cupped his hand behind his ear. "I'm a little deaf."

"You live in Caratunk?" my friend relayed my question, as he was nearer to the open window and the gangly man standing there.

"No, I'm from Bingham," he replied as he wiped sweat from his balding head and placed his walking stick in the cab of his truck.

"I use'ta drive all the way from Pleasant Pond to The Forks years ago," he said without missing a beat—then, pointing north on the road, he added, "How many camps down the road there now?"

"Well, there's five on the Hangtown road and two on the Crossover Road," my friend replied.

"Is that right? There's a cellar-hole somewhere out on the Divide road. Saw it a few years back," he related.

Feeling sorry for him as he swiped at another fly, we bade him a good-day and turned onto the Crossover road to clear any trees fallen from the latest storm.

We didn't get but a few yards when I said, "we should have asked him if he knew how Hangtown got its name. He really seemed to know a bit of history of the area."

My friend, abruptly turned the ATV around. We caught the man removing a sheathed, long-bladed knife from his belt just as he was about to climb into his truck.

"Hey, by any chance do you know how Hangtown got its name?" I blurted out.

Throwing the sheathed knife onto the front seat, he drawled. "Wellll," as he studied us for a second or two. "I know the real story, but I'm not sure about telling it in front of a lady," he added, looking quizzically at me with an uncertain and somewhat toothless smile.

"P'ff, don't let that stop you," I returned with an eager smile, deducing more information for my book. I did not mention that I was researching the history of Hangtown.

So, he continued, "Sometime around the 1900s a tramp came up here. You know, there were a lot of tramps around in those days— wand'ring around and holdin' up in farmer's barns and so on. Well, one of those tramps raped a homesteader's daughter and the homesteader found him and hung him. There was word of the deed and that got back to the sheriff in Bingham. The sheriff came up to investigate, bringin' dogs to search for the body, but no luck . . . never did find the body—no body—no arrest."

[In 1921, Daily Kennebec Journal published an article defining three vagrant classes: The tramp being The younger fellow who works a little and travels a great deal; the bum, who drinks a great deal and works a little, and the hobo, who works a little, drinks a little and travels a little.]

As my eyebrows raised, my friend said, "Probably more than one body around up here. Have to be careful where we dig for gravel," as he glanced my way.

"Yup, I imagine the homesteaders buried more than one baby up here under some of those big rocks," the gentleman offered. "A lot of children died up here and I don't imagine they buried them all down there as he points downhill toward Caratunk. There were quite a few homesteaders here before the machinery came," The old man continued.

I couldn't help asking if he knew when the farms were abandoned.

"Well," he wiped his brow again, "when the machinery and car era came. There was no money in homesteadin'— just survival. People just raised what they needed to live on. Big families back then too. Everyone worked on the farm. Hard work and the land so rocky. Good for potatoes tho' and hay. A lot of hay back in those days. Potatoes was quite the staple. Gave it all up they did—could make more money in the cities, better livin', money to buy luxury things—like cars. You know, homesteaders had no money—just provided what they needed for survival. No frivolities."

It all made sense to me, yet I wondered how many of those home-steads were lost because husbands went away to war or logging, with many injured or not returning at all. The wives and children, with many too young to help, were left to work the farms–yet couldn't!

Although I had many more questions for him, it was time to let this fly-molested gentleman take refuge in his truck. We said goodbye to our new acquaintance and continued on our way, only to realize that I hadn't asked for his name. Ah, more research—to find this man again!

During my research into the origin of the local 'Hangtown' name, historian and author Marilyn Sterling-Gondek, proposed an intriguing theory. She suggested that during their time serving in the army, James Powell Sr. and young James may have been stationed in or near Placerville, California—once infamously known as Hangtown. Hangtown, where three men (possibly more) were hanged in 1849, was renamed Placerville in 1854. Howwever, the townspeople continued to call it Hangtown—exploiting the town's notorious history. Sterling-Gondek thought perhaps

Powell had impulsively nicknamed his farming community Hangtown—and the name just stuck with the neighbors.

After discovering the article Nugget's Luck, printed in the journal in 1898, I theorize that Powell and others read it and fittingly adopted the name. To further expound on that article, may I remind you, Placerville, originally known as 'Hangtown', was first called Dry Diggings. What better description could our farmers give for tilling the rocky soil for strawberries, vegetables, hay, and the multitude of potatoes grown and harvested, other than dry diggings. This, combined with the following local lore, reveals how 'Hangtown' and the 'Hangtown Road.' most likely acquired their names.

The origin of this next explanation is unknown but passed to me via a previous resident of The Forks' Hangtown.

Years ago, maybe early 1900s, some young children decided one evening to raid a neighbor's strawberry patch of the delicious ripe berries. They were caught and a mock trial was set up with neighboring farmers joining in. These farmers counted on the crops they worked so hard to raise—food that kept their families fed and brought in a little money—money they could not spare. When the 'court of farmers' was held, it was decided to teach the children a lesson. After quizzing the young group, the mock court found them guilty and sentenced them to death by hanging. Shocked and frightened, the youngsters promised never to steal again. The 'court of farmers' showed leniency and sent them home to their parents for further punishment!

A similar story, handed down through generations from a local postmaster, follows:

Back in the late 1800s there were quite a few farms and open fields along the Road from Pleasant Pond to The Forks—quite a settlement north of Holly Brook. This area became known as Hangtown. There were farms with substantial gardens—hay, oats and wheat-producing fields. Gardens were a big thing back then—people lived off the land—that was all they had. Many of the farmers started losing vegetables, fruits and even tools from their gardens, barns and sheds. Local word filtered out to the Sheriff and upon arrival to the community he was confronted by the local farmers. They unconditionally stressed that they took care of their own problems. With that the sheriff departed. The problem continued with the stealing getting worse each night until a number of the farmers hid in their barns to see who was responsible. They discovered it was kids doing the stealing and decided to give them a lesson which they hoped the kids would never forget. The farmers got together and secretly built a gallows. After rounding up the delinquent children, they were brought to the gallows and made to climb the stairs. Hoods and nooses were placed on each child as they were asked if they had any words, apologies, or prayers. The children were crying and shaking, thinking the end was near. However, the farmers finally released them, charging them to never steal again. One would hope they never did!

The props are all here. The article published in 1898 embellishes the history of California's Hangtown—thievery, hanging, dry diggings—all staged for a new Maine Hangtown full of mirth, intrigue and folklore, creating inevitable questions!

The mind can run wild with anxiety, imagination, and embellished rumors—what amusement for some!

The Hangtown noose came down in 2018 along with the old Balm in Gilead Tree. The old tree, with a circumference of thirteen feet seven inches when measured at four feet above the ground, just gave up. Its roots were ripped from the ground by Mother Nature and her merciless powerful wind. I can only think of it as a beautiful, kind old tree that fell gracefully. Its massive branches kissed the edge of my porch roof, taking just three new asphalt shingles. Its rugged top nearly demolished my friend's 2008, 3130 Kubota tractor leaving a large dent in its previously unscathed hood!

*Image 8. Balm of Gilead tree in front
of cabin. Photo by the author.*

Image 8b. Balm of Gilead tree and tractor. Photo by the author.

For a while the noose hung on my porch as a reminder to research the history of Hangtown and those families who once lived here. However, as with Placerville, censure won in 2020 with the removal of the old noose that once hung in that ancient Balm in Gilead tree. No one seems to know where it ended up.

Chapter 16

GHOSTS IN HANGTOWN

Do THE STORIES of the noose perhaps bring on the thoughts of ghosts? Did people believe that those hanged were still wandering? Were mothers and babies searching for each other? Some did for sure, as I was asked not long after I had bought my camp, if anything strange was happening?

"Like what?" I asked.

"There are ghosts said to be in Hangtown, everyone knows that," a local confided in me one day, "Ghosts wandering around the old foundations and Holly Brook have been seen!"

"For real?" I query, as she definitely had my attention.

"I have even heard that people often go to Hangtown to call up the spirits," she added.

I left with a new found curiosity and many questions. Are there ghosts in Hangtown? It was time to delve into the mystery. Regardless of whether there are ghosts or not, I began inquiring with other camp owners and local townspeople.

One individual related that while camping just off the Hangtown Road, he heard voices, laughter, screeching, and saw blinking lights as a group of six people meandered down the road from the north. They reached the old Sizeland farm, seating themselves on rocks circling the old foundation while holding flickering candles. The camper had slipped down through the woods watching and listening to the eerie low murmurs of the group. He related how they only stayed a short time then filed away still talking in low tones.

Other camp owners have told me that after hearing voices they crept through the dark woods to watch and listen as visitors performed their meetings. I was told that the visitors gathered at the old foundations especially on the weekends close to Halloween. Séances were performed as the moon silhouetted the intruders. Sometimes the observers could see a group with a Ouija board, their fingers on the planchette moving about to spell out the name or message. Often, the board was seen flying through the air as the players reacted to the spirit. Fluttering candles and flowing white sheets were used to reach out to spirits—or to mock them—depending on the individual. The next day, items such as burnt candles and cards could be found scattered on the ancient ground, as if someone had been chased away—perhaps by the very spirits they had conjured.

And yes, some of the spirits must have been summoned, as believed by an old logger back around 1995. He was doing some work for one of the summer residents on the Hangtown Road and left quite abruptly one warm autumn night.

The job was quite a distance from his home so he moved his camper to a friend's place on the north end of the Hangtown Road. He had gone to bed after a full day of logging. Around two in the morning he noticed his sheet had been stripped from his tired body. Thinking he had been dreaming, tossing, and turning, he pulled the sheet up settling in for a few more hours of sleep. The sheet was stripped off again. Cautiously and now pretty much awake he pulled it up again. The third time he was not even close to sleep as the sheet was pulled away. He jumped up, grabbed his clothes, and beat it for home. A few days later, he returned for his camper; taking no time in loading it, and, as he put it, 'getting to hell outta there.'

A few years later this same man and his wife returned to Hangtown to spend the weekend with his friends who had now built a camp where he had camped before. As he and his wife settled into bed, the wife experienced a hand touching her chest. She immediately blamed it on her husband and told him so. He thought she was crazy and telling her so!

Of course their conversation could be heard in the adjoining bedroom with that couple, quietly snickering, knowing what was coming next.

Once again the hand rested on the wife's chest and she again cussed her husband. He yelled out that it was not him. Remembering what had happened with the sheets before, they threw back the covers, jumped out of bed, grabbed their clothes and ran out of the camp, jumped into their car and headed for home. The camp owners tried to coax the couple back admitting to the hoax but the attempt was fruitless. The couple were not convinced, and never returned to Hangtown!

Some, really did believe Hangtown was haunted as did a plumbing inspector back in the mid 90's . . . that's 1990s. The camp owner relayed how he would wake with the feeling that someone was sitting on the edge of the bed. When he opened his eyes, no one was there.

"Don't know why anyone would want to build a camp up here—the place is haunted," the inspector barked. Hurriedly getting into his car, he growled, "I'll send you the paperwork."

As the local contractor arrived to install the grey water system he cautioned, "Don't cha know, everyone knows this place is haunted; has been for years." as he glanced back at the camp. "These were the biggest fields around here." said the contractor, "ya never know what's under them rocks out there."

Another seemingly victim, related how he was staying in his truck camper while building on the old Sizeland property. Every night around two a.m. he heard pounding.

"I tell you, it's like someone pounding on ledge," he describes to me as he adjusts his cap, "every night!"

Other camp owners claimed they had seen ghosts. While others experienced things such as missing items that later reappeared—a drifting of white caught by an unsuspecting eye—a hand coming to rest on that of a sleeping victim awakening her and softly calling her name—a face that when acknowledged shrinks from all sides to nothing before it can be identified—the howling when there is no wind.

Although rumors have it that many children and other unidentified bodies lay amongst the piles of stones found here and afield, there is of course no substantial proof here, and will not be unless a spirit wakes or the stones are thrown about.

The Field Ghosts

One tale told to me was about a logger from the 1990s I'll call Austin.

Austin dragged himself out of bed, yawning and nearly tripping over the dog lying at the foot of his bed. Champ, a big, playful St. Bernard, was stretching, ready to follow his master to breakfast—he hoped. Not wanting to get bowled over by his dog, Austin watched as Champ nearly rolled down the stairs and headed for the door. He pushed past the big fur ball, unlatched and kicked open the always-stuck kitchen door, mumbling to himself, "Someday I'll fix that thing." Champ rushed out heading for the neighbor's yard. "Damn dog," Austin thought as he headed for the bathroom. "Just what I need, another complaint from her," he fumed. "She oughta get a dog; then she'd know how it is," he said aloud.

After taking care of his own business, washed up and ready to roll, he grabbed one of his mother's cinnamon-sugar-topped blueberry muffins, stuffed it in his mouth, and yanked open the door. There stood his slobbering dog, fresh from a thirst-quenching drink at the nearby spring. Champ sniffed and licked muffin crumbs off the floor as Austin slapped himself on the forehead, remembering he hadn't fed the dog yet! Champ brushed through the door, sniffed his dish, his tail wagging slowly as if to ask—what the . . . ?

After filling the dish, it was empty within seconds. At the same time, they squeezed through the door, Austin slamming it shut behind him as Champ sprang into the bed of the pickup truck.

Running late again, Austin jumped behind the wheel, threw it in reverse, and backed out of the driveway without hesitation. He slammed it into drive as Champ first bounced forward, then back, thudding against the closed tailgate. It was a challenge for Champ to keep his paws under him on the frantic drive, but finally, with no injuries to him or the truck, they reached the log yard.

Once tilled fields, they are now overgrown with pine and fir trees, leaving only a small dry-grass field around the old farm. It was these trees that Austin had to cut and haul to the roadside. Parking his truck, he looked at the old farmhouse, wondering how long it had been abandoned. "No time to think about it now," he reckoned, as he opened the tailgate for Champ. Eager to get started, Austin leapt onto the Kubota tractor, grabbed the key, expecting the machine to fire right up—but not this time. A click was all he got. A little tap on the battery terminal with his trusty chainsaw wrench was all it needed. On the next turn of the key, the old girl sputtered to life.

Champ, as always, made his way around the edge of the woods marking his territory—a time-consuming daily ritual. He spent hours sniffing around the old farmyard, and some mornings he'd just lie on the slanted-roof porch. Made himself right ta home, he did!

When Austin hauled logs, Champ knew to keep out of the way. Experience had taught him that logs can roll and pups can get hurt. He learned another lesson too. Whenever his master started that roaring saw he tucked his tail and trotted back to his safe haven, the truck. There, he would peek around the edge of the cab with drool running down both sides of his muzzle, creating patterns on the sides of his master's cab. He would never forget that spine-chilling day.

He remembered the crack, followed by the whoosh as the tree

came crashing down, pinning him to the ground and its branches obscuring his vision as he frantically scanned for his master. He heard his master's voice coming closer and closer. Finally he felt his presence and smelled his sweaty scent even before he heard his name. "Champ, hang on buddy, you ok?" his master yelled out. Champ answered with a small wine and a throttled woof, and as the roar of the chainsaw filled his ears, he watched branches drop from the tree. Champ could now see his master as Austin knelt to check his dog's condition. "You OK, buddy?" Austin repeated, relieved to find Champ was alive and well, observing the squirming and the tail wagging,

Austin was digging a path to get to Champ as Champ wiggled and pushed with his hind feet to get to him. Champ, was finally out, and before Austin could get up, his buddy rushed him with all his weight, knocking him flat on the ground. Champ stood over his master bathing his face in slobbery licks! "Okay, okay," Austin laughed. "Enough is enough!" Austin chuckled feeling his tension ease.

What a lucky dog he was. There was a hollow in the forest floor where Champ stood which saved him. When the tree came crashing down, it flattened him into that hollow, while its now-bent branches pressed against the forest floor, holding its weight off Champ.

The next time Champ heard the chainsaw, he sneaked away and trotted all the way home. Austin had found him sitting by the kitchen door with just the tip of his tail wiggling. He knew Austin was not pleased with him as his master slammed the truck's door. Austin punished him by locking him in the house while he went back to work. The next day, Champ was left home alone again. Champ would not hear of it the third day. When he was let out that morning for his morning rituals, he sat by the truck, refusing to return to the house. Austin smiled to himself, as he opened the tailgate for his best friend. "See that you stay with me today," he growled at Champ, playfully cuffing his head. From that day on, Champ stayed at work. However, if Austin started the saw, Champ would run to the truck and jump in the back. The tailgate was always left down for him.

Now, today, Austin headed for the trees he had cut yesterday, opening to the field around the old farmhouse. What a shame, he thought, to let the place die like that.

The old farm, now abandoned and surrounded by forest, was a picture of days gone by. What had once been a working farm: a barnyard full of chickens, ducks, and hens was now silent in the morning mist. The whispering fields of hay, oats, corn and potatoes and so much more were now overgrown with pine-scented trees and rustling brush. The horses and oxen, with their pungent, musky odor, have been replaced with tractors, skidders, and trucks spewing diesel fumes as they invade the forgotten land. The old farmhouse, along with its attached sheds and barn, are now slumped with the weight of age.

Austin sighed with resignation. How he longed to step back in time, to farm this land, work for himself, and raise crops, animals, and a family of his own. Oh well, he thought, I've got my old tractor and my loyal dog, what more should I want? With that he goosed the throttle on the old sputtering tractor and headed to hitch up some pine logs.

It had been a good day. Austin and Champ had stopped for lunch around noonish. Austin never kept good time or a schedule—Champ usually told him when lunch time was. They sat on one of the logs Austin had cut. Austin slapped his sandwich down on the log as he reached for his Classic Coke. Champ moved in closer to sniff the fat sandwich, unstoppable drool dripping from both corners of his open mouth. His master grabbed the sandwich just before Champ could snatch it! 'Damn dog,' Austin thought as he pulled off a piece and gave it to him. With one gulp, it was gone. Champ moved on to his water dish, knowing he wasn't getting any more.

The rest of the day was spent swinging the chain saw. Austin would cut the tree down, limb it, measure and cut it to length for the mill. 'Time to call it a day,' he thought. Tomorrow he'd start by hauling the logs out to the roadside, stacking them with the others for the logging truck to load and haul to the mill.

Champ was in a playful mood the next morning and very early he decided to wake his master. Placing both paws on Austin's bed, he delivered a big sloppy tongue-slurp right across his face. That stopped the snoring. "You big goofy hound—it's not even six yet," Austin complained as he jumped out of bed, wrestling Champ out of the way while shuffling to the bathroom. "Might as well go to work," he grumbled.

With the morning routine completed, they headed out the door for work. It was damp and misty outside and Champ decided he was riding inside today. Austin couldn't blame him, so he threw the dog blanket across the back seat. "Get in there, you big brute, and keep the drool to yourself," he said good-naturedly. Smiling he got into the cab, backed out of the driveway and headed to work.

It was a damp, foggy day with just enough promise of sun where things might dry out. Austin backed up to the logs for his second twitch of the day. Getting off, he climbed down and grabbed the choker chains. He hooked them around his logs, winched them up with the cable, and set the brake before climbing back on the tractor, and heading for the roadside.

Champ hadn't wanted to leave the truck where he was warm and dry. But with the sun beating in on him and his master out by the roadside, now was time for him to make his rounds.

The sun was brighter now, with the fog lifting as Austin returned, allowing him to see the outlines of the old fields, edged with piles of rocks barely visible beneath moss and the dead grasses. The old fencing, some still standing, with parts ripped and yanked down by years of twining grasses and tangling vines painted a picture of neglect.

The empty truck caught Austin's eye prompting him to scan the forest's edge and the fields. Assuming Champ was snooping around as usual, he turned his attention back to hooking up another twitch. As he rose from securing the first choker, a movement caught his eye— Champ racing towards the old farmhouse. Suddenly Champ stopped. His wagging tail slowly stilled, then drooped. Lowering his head, his ears sagging, and tail tucked between his legs, he turned and trotted back to Austin, leaning against his master's leg. Austin glanced back to see what was spooking his dog.

What appeared to be a son, father, mother, and daughter stood side by side, about two hundred feet from the old farmhouse. They were dressed in older-looking clothes, the women wearing long breeze-swaying dresses. Standing ahead of the group was a tall, black-and-tan dog. Its stance suggested a watchful protection for his family. "Weird," Austin thought turning back to his twitch, "I'll go see what they're up to when I get back from this load," he concluded. "How strange," Austin pondered as he hauled his logs towards the road. "That Champ had not rushed up to them." Champ loved socializing with both people and dogs. This wasn't like him at all. With that thought, Austin glanced back and spotted Champ in the truck, sitting upright with an intense stare fixed on the field from where he had ran. Following his dog's fixation on the field, Austin looked up—but there was no one in sight.

Wondering where they had come from and how they'd disappeared so quickly left Austin with more questions than answers. There was only one way onto the farm and that road was blocked by his logs. He made up his mind to ask his boss and the trucker if they'd seen these people before. Maybe the owner was selling the place.

Austin finished the day with six twitches and a few more trees cut. Neither his boss nor the trucker had seen anyone around the old farm, and as far as they knew it was not up for sale. Champ seemed more like himself once they were headed back towards town. Back home he couldn't wait to get out of the truck. Jumping out, he made a beeline for the neighbor who was sitting on the steps enjoying the sunshine. Austin, his arms full, plopped the groceries on the truck's hood as he ran after his dog. "Shit," he breathed. "She's out here." He rolled his eyes, but no one noticed. Champ was oblivious to Austin's presence, as he sped by to retrieve the ball she had thrown. The girl, however, wasn't; she walked up to Austin offering her hand.

"Hi, I'm Annie, your neighbor," she said, smiling and adding, "the one you see scooping up after our friend here."

Embarrassed and a little agitated, Austin grabbed Champ and muttered, "Sorry 'bout that. I try, but he's got a mind of his own," he added as he struggled to drag the 190 pound muscle-bound brute back home. Annie bursts out laughing handing the tennis ball to Austin.

"Try this," she said with a mischievous smile, while Champ sat intently watching the action between his master and Annie.

"Not a bad idea," Austin chuckled much more at ease.

"You want a beer?" Annie asked. Austin nodded and the conversation shifted from light banter to everyday matters.

Annie offered to watch Champ anytime Austin had to go to work, explaining that she was a writer and stayed home all day anyway. Austin expressed his gratitude, adding that he worked in the woods and always took Champ with him. He described how he harvested trees for his boss, who had contracts with landowners wanting timber cut from their properties. Annie frowned, recalling how she had heard Champ howling for two days while Austin was away. Curious, she asked about it, and Austin quickly filled her in on the chainsaw incident that had occurred on the old farm.

Annie perked up with great interest, hearing Austin speak of the old farm and wanting to learn more. He explained that his job was to cut trees that had overtaken old farmland, which was once part of a small community. It was pretty remote, accessed only by an old county road—now a woods road.

Annie, taking it all in, noticed a shift in Austin's demeanor. Confused and remembering his workday's unsettling experience with the vanishing family, Austin felt compelled to relate the incident to Annie. Annie listened, sensing something eerily familiar about Austin's descriptions of the farm and the supposed family he had witnessed. Rising, she excused herself momentarily before returning with an old framed photograph which she handed to Austin. He looked at the sepia-toned photo. Sucking in his breath, he shifted his gaze to Annie.

"Who are they, Annie?" he asked faintly, experiencing a slight chill. Champ, who had been sleeping, moved closer to him, sensing a swing in his master's mood.

"My ancestors, Austin," Annie said, her voice barely above whispering. "They owned that farm," she said softly, adding, "It's mine now."

Champ looked from Austin to Annie, contented, he then laid down and, with his chin resting on his paws, went to sleep.

Holly Brook Ghosts—They Never Seem to Rest

Anyone passing through the hollow at Holly Brook after dusk learns why the stories persist.

A brisk walk—for it was getting quite dark and he had at least another half mile to go. The hollow at Holly Brook was his biggest fear. He wouldn't have even been out here this late if it weren't for needing to harvest his crop before someone else did- just like last year. All the work he had put in last year and some jerk had reaped the benefits!

Moving right along, soon he was at the top of the hill where the old schoolhouse used to be. He stumbled over the deep ruts and exposed boulders in the road. His breath came rapidly now with his hurried movements and adrenalin was building fast as he anticipated the rest of his journey.

Hesitating he listened. Catching the slightest gurgling of what he hoped was the brook making its way over and around the always slippery rocks that he knew so well. He didn't mind wading and dipping in the cool waters there at Holly Brook during daylight but it was when the light faded that hairs would stand up on the back of his neck and every normal sound became abnormal. The haunting would start.

The old wooden bridge, worn by the heavy log trucks and winter trail groomers, creaked only after dark or was that his imagination? The gurgling would become even more evident leaving foam on those slimy rocks and ghostly vapors would form above the brook, suspend for seconds and whisk away. He knew this. He had seen. He moved on more quickly now.

A loud snap made him freeze. It was then he heard the eerie moan; the rustling alders, and swooshing of air that met his cheek. Startled he nearly dropped his botanical load. It was not heavy but oh the pungent smell really should ward off the mosquitoes attacking him he thought.

Low flying bats scooping mosquitoes into their tail and wing membranes swooped all around him. Heart pounding he swung his bushy bundle at them as his strangled screams escaped his trembling lips. Hurriedly he stumbled on towards the brook. As he stood debating whether to ford the brook or trust the bridge again the eerie moan and breath of gentle air was enough to make him rush across the old lopsided bridge.

He dared not look back, however, he could not fight the urge to do so. Childhood memories of Ichabod Crane was too real to him at this moment. No moon was out tonight, just misty rain nearly obscuring the forest. He was sure he could hear pounding of feet yet he suspected it was his heart instead. Assuring himself that this was not Sleepy Hollow and there would be no headless horseman he turned to trudge up the steep hill. Soon, he hoped to be home.

As he neared the crossover from the Appalachian Trail, sudden movement caught him off guard—he dropped his load—running back down the hill. A voice halted his descent bringing him up short—one boot still held in the air. Turning slowly he saw that it was just a hiker who seemed surprised to see him as well. Neither noticed the slight and light apparition fade behind the tall pine.

❧

She watched the two men as they nervously laughed at their cowardly behavior. She often wondered why people acted nervous and afraid at Holly Brook. Perhaps she should have, all those years ago when she was sent away from home. She could not remember why. After spending so much time in the hospital she was finally allowed to come home again. How she loved to walk through the woods and spend hours at the brook. Sometimes fishing sometimes just daydreaming—even knowing she was ignoring her household duties and demands of her family. The second time she was sent away she decided to leave that hospital place forever. She would never go back. She would drink her potion.

She found peace again at the Brook and no one could take her away now. It was hers as long as she kept her apparition from being seen. That was not easy for there were others who came here as well.

She had seen them the day she had arrived from the Home. She had watched as a lady stopped on the bridge throwing something into the brook below. She could not tell what as it floated under the bridge. As it appeared on her side, she saw a beautiful bouquet of white roses. Spinning and dipping, dancing around the stones in the brook, they finally fetched up further down, resting there, bouncing in a shallow pool. The lady, with tears streaming down her cheeks, slowly turned and wandered north along the trail.

She could not help herself from following—she had seen this woman before—if only she could remember- but that is what got her in this state to begin with: she could not remember, and was sent away.

Now, fearing she had wandered too far from her Holly Brook, she quickly swooped back to her trusted pines and floated down to the water. There at the rose-filled pool, a tiny apparition hovered, weeping and grasping the flowers as it faded from the Brook.

She saw many after this. Some were mischievous as they swooped down in front of dogs or when they whispered in hikers ears. The wandering hiker often collapsing his tent as he rushed from it in fear. There were many like her here at Holly Brook for sure.

As she drifted upwards, again she watched the two men as one crossed the road and continued east on that Appalachian Trail—as they called it now. She remembered Marion Hill living not far from there . . . not far at all.

The other man now gingerly bent down and picked up his green bundle, quickly looked behind him as he tripped forward gathering himself just in time avoiding a harsh tumble. Shaking his head he continued uphill glancing sideways now and again as if sensing someone or something walking beside him. The woods were dark now, the trees hanging over the road, rain dripping off his visor obscuring his vision while magnifying his fears. He remembered that night when he awoke to a loud moan reaching to nearly a screech and the rattling of the window where he caught the slightest ghostly shadow. It had to be a phantasmal image- he would not consider any other explanation. With his big mag light he had nervously crept through the rooms, checking windows and doors and behind doors with shadows intensifying his overactive imagination. He finally calmed himself, resolving that it was just a gust of wind that had disrupted his sleep that night—or so he wanted to believe.

He must calm himself now, for he was not home yet. It troubled him that whenever he was near Holly Brook he sensed uneasiness, restlessness, tension or turmoil. He couldn't really put his finger on it but it certainly seemed to effect his angst. The burden of his load was nothing compared to the hovering panic he was experiencing. Much to do from the stories he had heard about the Ghosts in Hangtown. More than one acquaintance had expressed concern for his wellbeing when they heard he was living in Hangtown. They had related how they had seen ghostly images around the old foundations and hovering over the piles of rocks deep in the woods. Rocks placed as if they were covering bodies. Some camp owners had tools that disappeared and later found them in very odd places such as the bottom of the deep spring, behind his place, and items hanging from the old Balm of Gilead tree.

Pleasant Ponders walked the Old Hangtown Road but would speedily return home before dark, as they believed the spirits would then be present. Some walked with dogs that became spooked when crossing the Holly Brook Bridge. Their tails hung as they pressed against their owner's legs seemingly for protection. He knew! He, too, had experienced this with his own dog.

Finally, he turned into his driveway. Looking up towards his camp, now his home, there was a soft glow of flickering light. His mind racing as his feet wished to do, the light became brighter. It took a few prolonged minutes before he realized he had left a gas light on for his return. That's it he had had enough. The wind was howling now and the icy rain continued to beat down on him. He would not spend another windy night in Hangtown—never!

◈

Drifting between the swaying pine trees she watched as his car bumped over the Holly Brook Bridge. With spinning tires on the loose stones in the road the red lights soon disappeared over the hill, leaving all quiet until the haunting laughter shattered the silence.

Wanting to take no part in this prankish behavior, she slipped away—her ethereal figure lost amongst the towering pines.

◈

The tranquil forest offered a stark contrast to the lively and untold stories that could be told of Holly Brook!

But seriously, in the mid-1800s, the 'modern spiritualist' movement started. It is believed to initially have started in New York with the Fox Sisters in 1848. They were fourteen and eleven years old when they first started experiencing the hearing of knocking on walls, furniture moving, stomping. They found they could communicate with the spirits. Eventually they started sharing their abilities, and a modern spiritualist movement began. The timing of this movement seemed to be further fueled by the growing technology of photography and also by the Civil War.

The new technology in photography could produce ghostly images allowing people to believe that their loved ones were near; even though they could not see, hear, or touch them. The Civil war brought on an abundance of followers for this gave them a chance to speak to their loved ones through a medium or séances. The hope was to confirm that the lost were at peace, and give closure to the living.

The Movement raced through towns, cities and states. The Forks was no different and their own Myra French, millinery store owner and spiritualist, was a delegate from the Madison Spiritualist Camp, on Hayden Pond—known today as Lake Wesserunsett— in Lakewood. As delegate, in 1898, she attended the National Association of Spiritualists at Washington, D.C.

With so many loved ones dying, some turned from religious beliefs seeking a new meaning and answers to the vigils of life. Meetings and séances were held in community buildings or in an individual's home, as the Spiritual meeting Mrs. Barker conducted at The Forks in April, 1921.

Imagine being able to speak to your deceased loved one . . . once more—just to be able to voice those dear words that often go unspoken: "I love you".

Yes, so many died very young back then that no wonder people were looking for the spirits. Spirits not wanting to leave—mothers hoping to hear the sweet voices of their children—children wanting for their parents. People searching for their history and ghosts of their ancestors.

Don't believe in Ghosts? Well, there was Paddy McGee who kept the neighbors alert and children behaving!

Chapter 17

PADDY MCGEE

Patrick 'Paddy' McGee was a character in the early 1900s who lived in a shack, at the south beach area of Pleasant Pond. His sister, Lisa Collins, owned a cottage on the North Beach of the Pond. Pleasant Pond was well known to fisherman, including those from Hangtown who not only spent time fishing but visiting family, friends, and neighbors in the area.

Paddy McGee was Irish and was 'squatting' on land that he claimed the Township had given to him. From the 1900 census information, McGee's birthplace was Canada. He was the head of household; estimated at 42 years old; and single. His father and mother were Irish Canadian. It was noted that he could not read or write and that he was squatting on the land. I found it hard to read the census agent's writing. Some columns were left empty and others hurriedly filled, as if the agent, Virgil Hall, could not wait to get out of McGee's presence.

A misanthropist, McGee abhorred and distrusted humans. The locals found him peculiar and left him alone. However, many stories were told of this feared, eccentric hermit. It was said that he had two sets of teeth and children who misbehaved were threatened to be taken to him for punishment.

[From the book: The Upper Kennebec Valley,
by Jon F. Hall, Arcadia Publishing, 1997, pg. 33.
This book also has a picture of his shack. The
person outside appears to be a women and
not Paddy. Perhaps his sister, Lisa Collins.]

Rumors had it that he would chase off strangers and sometimes shoot at them. An article in the Independent- Reporter July 24, 1919 headlined, "Hermit Held For Shooting With Intent To Kill," confirms his behavior.

The article goes on to say that the hermit, Paddy McGee, who says he has lived at Pleasant Pond for thirty years, and claimed that the entire Township had been given to him, was arrested Tuesday, July 22, 1919. The complaint was made by John Lander, a wealthy lumberman formally of Bingham; residing in Boston and summering at Pleasant Pond. Landers alleged that McGee shot at him and a friend, Zikiel Butler, while they were boating. Being unable to get any of the Pond residents to assist in transporting them, Deputy Sheriff Robert Cole, accompanied by Deputy Elmer Adams of Madison and Frank Gipson of Bingham, rowed across the pond to McGee's camp. McGee at first refused arrest but later decided it best to comply.

In court, McGee admitted the shooting and claimed he fired behind both boats because they were making so much 'racket' that he, Paddy, 'would make some.'

"McGee was bound over in the sum of $2000 to appear at September term of Court. He was committed to jail," reports The independent-reporter, July 24, 1919.

On September 22, 1919, the case was taken care of by special order with no indictment by reason of insanity. Many disagreed with this determination and insisted that Paddy was not insane. However, Paddy McGee was transported to the Augusta State Hospital on Monday, October 7, 1919.

On the Feature Page of The independent-reporter issue of November 15, 1923, an article "Hermits of the Timber Region," includes McGee as one of the hermits and confirmed his incarceration in the "Hospital." Further searching for Paddy McGee brought nothing to light.

Chapter 18

MOVING INTO THE 1900S

The Hangtown Settlement

MOVING INTO THE 1900s, many of the earlier farmers were still residing in Hangtown. As the years crept forward, some of the homesteads were sold, some continued as farms, and others were bought for the timberland.

William E. Sizeland, who arrived in 1898, owns the Lewis Martin farm #21 having bought it from Herbert Prince. Sizeland was born in 1855; and had served in WWI. More about Sizeland in chapter 20. Herbert M. Prince, was born in 1859 in Detroit to Walter and Elmira Prince. Herbert married Lewis Martin's widow, Mary J. (Routh), at The Forks on June 20, 1899, his first marriage and her second. Mary J. died November 11, 1901 of pelvic cancer and was buried at Webster Cemetery in Caratunk. Herbert died in 1945.

James Powell Jr. lives on his farm lot #29—which was once Lovejoy's farm. Powell purchased it from his step-father, William Adams. He also owned lot #20 until 1906. In 1909, he purchased 5 acres of land, including buildings—his old homestead—of lot #30, from Alanson Hunnewell.

David Devoll, earlier farming on Lovejoy's lot #20, had moved in 1888. The property was then purchased by William Adams and later sold to James Powell. In 1906 Powell sold this 100 acre (lot #20) to the lumbermen, Forsyth and Heath.

Seldon James Melvin sold his home and 1.5 acres to Ethel (Ethelred) Young in 1903. Ethel had also purchased another 114 acres from W.H Clark. Ethel and Mary had four children, Walter, Ivy, Fred and Flora. The Young's lives were always in turmoil with Mary's health. After nearly seven years of treatment at Chelsea (Togus) Hospital for insanity, Mary self-administered a fatal overdose of strychnine and passed away in March 1921. Ethel had already sold his land and buildings to Alanson Hunnewell the previous August, 1920.

The Pleasant Pond Settlement (the southern end of the Hangtown road)-

Justus Adams moved to Solon and sold his property to William H., and Omar Clark. Omar's share was subsequently distributed to nine others. Together, they and William sold the entire property to Alanson Hunnewell in 1921.

After Albert Spaulding relocated to Embden in 1900, he sold his property to Fred Clark who owned acres of land around Pleasant Pond and along the Pleasant Pond Road to the Old Moxie Road. Part of Spaulding's later becoming Bateman's.

Cyrus Williams moved to Bingham some time before 1870. The ownership of his property changed hands numerous times and finely was purchased by Alice Goodrich and Frank Taylor in 1900. Parts owned now by Paddock and Wing.

Anthony Comber bought 80 acres from Lewis Martin in 1891. The 80 acres boundaries were defined as: Justus Adams Lot, now owned by William H. Clark, being the north boundary. The East boundary was Albert Spaulding Lot. To the west was Edward Martin's Lot and the boundary on the South was the southern line of The Forks Plantation. It had once belonged to Jeremiah Hill.

Born in Canada, Anthony immigrated to the U.S. in 1889. He

married Katherine M. Her name was sometimes recorded as Mary C Comber; Catherine M Comber. Her maiden name was sometimes written as Sawler or Lawler. They had four children but only two lived to be adults; William H., and John J. Comber. Anthony was both a farmer and logger. He owned a team of horses and a complete logging outfit.

Around 1908, having obtained land from Fred Clark. Anthony built a large cottage at Pleasant Pond in Caratunk. In 1911, he passed away leaving his wife, Katherine, to execute his will. The will conveyed the farm and logging outfit, including buildings and livestock, to their son, William. A condition of the will allowed Katherine, to live there until her death.

Their second son, John J.—his wife was Barbara J. MacDonald—was deeded the 4 acres and cottage situated in Caratunk. John, a talented carpenter, built a home there in 1916. He rented out the one his father had previously built. John went on to construct four additional camps for rent.

When John's brother William passed away in 1931, his property in The Forks Plantation conveyed to John with the exception of the four parcels William had previously sold. These four parcels went to Elizabeth C. Grover, Martin Potter et al, Van Cleve H. Shuster, and Dwight Pease.

John's wife, Barbara, inherited the property upon John's death. She passed away, on January 1, 1989, leaving the property to their son, Hugh Comber. This was the same parcel as was conveyed to his uncle, William H. Comber, dated October 10, 1911.

In the early 1990s, Hugh Comber sold some of his property in The Forks to Jeff and Juanita McAllister and some to Jeff's brother, Ken.

[Hugh sold some of his Caratunk property on the North Shore to Milton D. Bates in 1990. In 1990, he also sold land in The Forks Plantation to Jeff and Juanita McAllister. In 1991, Hugh sold Ken a parcel of his property in The Forks Plantation; followed by two more in 1993.]

Hugh's brother, Wade, became the Conservator and Guardian of Hugh's estate in 1998, when Hugh became incompetent. Struggling with COPD for 15 years and following fourteen days of pneumonia, Hugh passed away intestate on April 16, 2002.

Chapter 19

SETTLER'S LOTS REVISITED

In 1907, Herbert Prince owner of lot #30 in Hangtown, became the first to sell his land to Alanson Hunnewell, the logger from Caratunk. In 1920, Tuttle, the owner of the Lawrence Hill lot # 26, sold his land and buildings to Hunnewell, as did Ethel Young the owner of lot #31. Jesse/Justus Adams homestead, on lot #33, was eventually sold to Hunnewell in 1921. James Powell was the last homesteader in Hangtown to sell to Hunnewell. He kept his one hundred-acre homestead, on lot #29, including his five acres of lot #30, until 1925. The last settler's property left in Hangtown was the William Sizeland's homestead, owned by his grandson, Elwin Sizeland. This one hundred-acre property, on Lot #21, was the only property in Hangtown that was not sold to Hunnewell. It was finally sold in 1986 to A.S. & C.B. Gould & Sons, Cornville.

Hunnewell owned the five lots until his death in 1961. He left them to Eva L. Webster, who was from Caratunk. Eva Webster owned them until her death, at which time she left these lots to her nieces, Lucille

F. McMullen, Dorothy W. Clark, and Virginia A. Bonner. In 1968, they sold Lot's 26, 29, 30, 31, and 33 (Hill's, Powell's, Hunnewell's, Young's, and Adams') to the Ethyl Corporation.

In 1967 Oxford Paper Company merged with Ethyl Corporation which originally operated as the Albemarle Paper Manufacturing Company in Virginia. Founded in 1887, Albemarle initially produced Kraft and blotter paper. In the 1950s, the company shifted its focus to plastic manufacturing. In 1962, Albemarle acquired the Ethyl Corporation, transforming it primarily into a distributor of tetraethyl lead, a fuel additive used to produce leaded gasoline.

In 1976, Ethyl Corporation conveyed its Maine holdings to Oxford Paper Company, a subsidiary of Boise-Cascade. In 1996, Oxford Paper Company conveyed the Maine holdings to Mead Oxford Corporation, which later changed its name to Meadwestvaco in 2003.

In 2003, Meadwestvaco conveyed its Maine holdings to Bayroot LLC., which are now managed by Wagner Forest Management. Today, we recognize Bayroot LLC as our Hangtown neighbors!

[Around 99 percent of Bayroot LLC, a Foreign Limited Liability Company, and 91 percent of Typhoon LLC, both owned by Yale University, which in turn owns more than 521,000 acres of land in the Unorganized Territory of Maine. Information from the 2019 data from Maine Revenue Services reports there are 9,284,166 acres of Unorganized Territory in Maine.]

All the lots in Hangtown were bought up by the paper companies except for Sizeland's, lot #21, which I will refer to as The 100 acres.

Chapter 20

HANGTOWN'S LAST OLD HOMESTEADER AND THE 100 ACRES

THESE 100 ACRES, which William E. Sizeland bought from Herbert Prince on November 16, 1898, stayed in Sizeland's family for 88 years and were not sold until 1986. This was originally Martin's old homestead, lot #21, with buildings that had already fallen into neglect. The other forsaken farms in the Hangtown area, as mentioned earlier, were sold one by one to logger Alanson Hunnewell.

William E. Sizeland was born in Ireland, December 1, 1855. As an immigrant from Ireland he arrived in the United States in 1872. From the obituary in the Bangor Daily News, April 18, 1934 it was noted that he had spent some time at sea. He eventually arrived in the West Forks, where he worked at The Forks Hotel sometime before the 1880 census. He was twenty-four years old, boarding with Elijah and Nancy Hill in the West Forks, as recorded on the 1880 census. Both William and Elijah were working as laborers. William married Lissie (Melissa) M. Young, of The Forks Plantation, in 1888. She was born in 1870.

William and Lissie had four children: Florence M. born June 1891, William 'Henry' E. born 1892, 'Baby Boy' Sizeland (date of death was 1895-no birth date), and Velma M. was born in 1898. A bit of interesting trivia: the tending physician was H.B. (Hulda) Young, Lissie's mother, and the clerk was E.R. Young, Lissie's brother.

*Image 9a. The Sizeland Farm. Photo
courtesy of William Henry Sizeland.*

Lissie died in 1899 after missing a step and falling onto the hard-packed cellar floor. She started hemorrhaging. The doctor was sent for—arriving just in time to stop the bleeding. However, soon after he left, Lissie began to hemorrhage again. Efforts were made to catch up with the doctor, but by the time he was brought back to the farm, Lissie had died. Her death certificate listed the cause as uterine hemorrhage. This left William to raise their three young children, ages eight, seven, and one. William away at work left his children with duties way beyond their years. Florence going on nine years old was left with the cooking, cleaning and also raising her one year old sister. Henry, only seven, was responsible for the barn chores along with chopping and lugging firewood, water and more. Somehow they did manage to attend school. Henry quit school when he was 14. He worked in the woods as a lumberjack earning a man's pay and turning it all over to his father to help with the expenses including the mortgage. Eventually, Henry was able to purchase a team of horses allowing him to earn more money as a teamster. With their hard work, the old farm saw new life with an addition onto the barn, more livestock, and the mortgage paid. All this time, William, along with Henry, made sure that Florence and Velma got the good educations they wanted.

Image 9b. William E. Sizeland. Photo courtesy of William Henry Sizeland.

Henry, was inducted into the Military at Skowhegan on May 28, 1918. He left for Camp Devens the following day. Private Sizeland departed for France on June 15, 1918 and was wounded at the front on October 4th. On October 11, he wrote to his father the following letter:

October 11, 1918

Dear Papa

Will write a few lines today to tell you I am alive and getting along fine. I was wounded October 4th in the left leg, left wrist, and right arm. But they are all flesh wounds so I will be just as good as ever as soon as they have time to heal. So don't worry any for we get the best of care in the hospital here. It's pretty weather here too but it was cold and rained all the time at the front. The first time I was at the front I never got a scratch.

How are you and the girls and Casper? Haven't heard a word from any of you yet. If you get this, write right straight back. Maybe I will get it before I leave the hospital. Get one of the girls to write to Cecilia for me. I will write her myself in a day or two but don't feel like it today.

How are you making it anyway and what are you going to do this winter? Hope the war will be over so I can be with you next winter. Do you ever hear from Winnie? I don't know where he is. Give my regards to all the neighbors. I wonder if you folks got all the letters I have written. Am getting tired so will close. Will write again soon. This is awful writing. Don't know as you can read it but my fingers are rather clumsy.

Love to all,

Henry

He added his address: Private Henry E. Sizeland at Base Hospital, Ward E.A.P.O. 785, American Expeditionary Forces.

—From The Independent Reporter, November 21, 1918.

[Cecilia later became his wife. Winnie (Winfield
Powell) a Hangtown neighbor of Henry's, served
in the war stationed behind the lines and cooking
in the officers' quarters. Later, in February 1919,
he was in France cooking on a train which was
transporting troops to the "seaport town".]

Private Sizeland sailed from France to New York on January 11, 1919. After arriving in New York, he wrote to his father about the rough voyage. February 6, 1919, Henry was honorably discharged.

Nearly a year later, on December 31, 1919, William "Henry" Sizeland married Ann Celia Leger. Both worked at a shoe factory in Auburn. Their first son, Earl F., was born in 1923 and their second son, Elwin H., was born in 1924.

William E. Sizeland remained on his sixty-year-old run-down farm until 1928. He moved from Hangtown to Bingham, where he lived with his daughter Velma and family. William E. died April 17, 1934 intestate. His wife, Lissie, had predeceased him by thirty-five years. William was buried in the Bean Cemetery alongside Lissie. He had owned The 100 Acres for 36 years.

The heirs of The 100 Acres, were Florence, Henry, and Velma. Henry became sole owner of The 100 Acres in 1949 when his two sisters, conveyed their shares to him.

It seems obvious that the farm was no longer inhabited with Sizeland's children having relocated to other towns and good paying jobs. The Forks Plantation's records show that somewhere between 1942 and 1944 the buildings were either collapsed or in such disrepair that they were deemed non-taxable.

About one-half of the land had been cleared for farming. Trees were still abundant on the rest of the property. It appears that some-time in the 1940s, Henry had more logging done on the property, perhaps by his good friend, Joe Beane. It appears at this time the farm-house and buildings were already collapsed.

Henry, owning The 100 Acres for 33 years—1934-1967, conveyed it to his oldest son, Earl, also of Auburn on December 12, 1967. William Henry E. Sizeland died at the age of seventy-seven in 1969.

Earl owned The 100 Acres from 1967-1983—16 years. He died leaving it to his brother, Elwin of Auburn. Elwin was also Earl's personal representative. The deed described surrounding neighbors as James Powell now Boise-Cascade to the north; Wm. H. Clark now Boise-Cascade to the East; Lawrence P. Hill now Boise-Cascade to the South; and Wm. H. Clark now Boise-Cascade to the West.

Elwin owned it for 3 years before he sold it in 1986 to A.S. and C.B. Gould & Sons, a logging company from Cornville, Maine. Elwin died at the age of 92 in 2017. His wife Geraldine died in 2020.

These 100 Acres were not divided until Gould sold 2.686 acres to Sacket and Brake Survey the following year. More about Gould's sales and the breakdown of these one-hundred acres in the next chapter.

As has become evident, this Hangtown farm of years ago is no longer around. This and the surrounding area can only boast a few camps, two year round residents, intermittent logging by Bayroot, LLC, seasonal hunting, snowmobiling, and yes, the well-known Appalachian Trail.

Chapter 21

WHAT BECAME OF THE NEXT GENERATION?

WHAT BECAME OF the last four families in Hangtown? The family farms were a lot of work with little benefits and it seems that none of the children wanted to take over the old farm. Only four Homesteads were left in Hangtown as the 1900s went forward: Powell's, Sizeland's, Young's, and Hill's.

The Hill Farm

The Lawrence Hill Farm was the first of these four farms to be somewhat abandoned. In 1917, he sold his homestead to Tuttle and Holeman from Athens. I found no record that either lived on that farm.

Hill's step-son, Benjamin Russell, first married Mary Elizabeth Powell, who died in 1890. He married Gertrude B. Pooler in 1894. They moved to Bingham where he worked as a farmer, carpenter, and later a millwright. They had three Children, Justin P., Kenneth S., and Marguerite Bertha. Apparently, Benjamin was a successful quide as evidenced by a picture in the Jan. 17, 1924, issue of the Independent Reporter showing him and his 'sports' beside a game pole with 10 deer and many partridge. At sixty years old, Benjamin worked as a carpenter at the Dam construction. Bingham remained his home until his death in 1948. His grave, along with Gertrude's, is located in the Bingham Village Cemetery.

It was difficult to trace Julia A. Russell's life through the later years. The reason being she was known as Annie, Angie, Anna, and sometimes Julianna. Julia was born in Smithfield. She was thirteen when they moved to Hangtown in 1880. At the age of seventeen she married James C. Martin, the Proprietor of the Pleasant Pond Hotel. Now known as Annie, she and James raised three children, Leroy, Daisy, and Inza. Daisy succumbed to pneumonia at age twenty-three. Eventually, James and Annie moved to Augusta where they owned a farm. James passed away at age fifty-nine in 1920. Annie moved to Solon to live with her daughter and son-in-law, Inza and Benjamin Miller. Annie passed away in Solon in 1941. She and James are buried in the Webster Cemetery.

Ethel Young's Farm

Ethelred Young and his wife, Mary A. Wintle, lived on their farm in Hangtown for seventeen years. Ethel sold his Hangtown homestead late in 1920 and apparently moved to Chelsea, on the east side of the Kennebec, near the Chelsea/Hallowell Ferry.

Their oldest child, Walter D., was born in 1902. At the age of seventeen and still living at home, he worked in a lumber mill, as recorded in the 1920 census. He moved to Sidney and worked as a farmhand for twenty years or more. From 1942 to 1943, he served as a private in the army during World War II. Late in life, he married Mildred Decrow, who was living in Belfast.

Walter's sister, Ivy M., was born in 1905. She graduated from Skowhegan high school June 1923, and continued her education at

Bates College. She apparently married a man named Hart. The last residence I found for her was recorded as Brooklyn, N.Y., and in 1951, she departed from New York on the SS Panama bound for Cristobal, Canal Zone.

The third child was Fred P. Young who was born in 1906. At the age of fourteen, he was already working on a farm and no longer attending school. By 1930, he was a farm laborer in Sidney, a role he seemingly continued into 1950, when he was still working as a farm laborer in Sidney alongside his brother, Walter. Fred P. Young never married and died at the age of fifty-seven in Waterville in 1963.

Flora Belle Young, the fourth child was born at home in 1910. Her Grandmother, Hulda B. Young, a midwife, delivered her at the family's home in Hangtown. In 1928, Flora married Aloysius J. Rogan, a widower thirty-eight years her elder, originally from New York. In 1918, he had purchased Annie Martin's Hotel at Pleasant Pond and was appointed postmaster there. Flora and Aloysius had one daughter, Caroline E. Rogan, in 1930. Rogan's property was foreclosed on by Albert Clark in 1942 and the Rogans relocated to Portland. Caroline married Ernest Howe in August 1950 in South Portland, Maine. By the 1950 census, Flora, now widowed, and her daughter are still residing in Portland where Flora is employed as an inspector in an industry. Flora at the age of eighty-six died in Portland in 1996. Her last recorded residence on the Social Security death index was in Roxbury, Maine, which was apparently where Caroline was living.

As said before, the Young homestead was sold to Alanson Hunnewell in 1920.

The Powell Farm

James and Lizzie Powell raised twelve children although two died early. Many were born at home. Where were their children in 1925, when James sold his homestead in Hangtown? What had become of his large family?

James E. Powell, the firstborn son of James and Lizzie Powell, was one month old when the 1870 census was recorded. Since no further record of him has been found, I assume he is one of the children who died earlier— sometime between 1870 and 1876.

Tracy Francis, their second son, was born in 1871. In 1893 Tracy married Cora L. Adams whose father was John Adams from The Forks. They made their home in Caratunk. They raised one child, Mildred A., born in 1903. Mildred succumbed to tuberculosis when she was just sixteen. Cora never recovered from the loss of her daughter. After being ill for three months, Cora passed away in Bingham Deveaux Hospital on March 20, 1924. She is buried in the Webster Cemetery.

Tracy moved to Springfield, Massachusetts. He remarried Rebecca A. (Staples) Powell. Tracy was a janitor for the Exeter building/apartments. Rebecca died in April 1934. Following her death and his own decline in health, Tracy became despondent. Just five months later, he committed suicide by inhaling gas from his kitchen stove. Rebecca is buried beside her mother's grave in Vermont. Tracy's grave is located in Caratunk's Webster Cemetery, beside Cora.

Mary Elizabeth was born in 1873. She married Benjamin H. Russell, Lawrence Hill's step-son, on December 3, 1890. They had one daughter, Mary A. Russell, who died at four months old. Mary Elizabeth died in 1890—yes, these are the dates found! Mother and daughter graves are at the Webster Cemetery.

David Eugene "Gene" Powell was born in 1875. Gene, was employed as a laborer and river driver. He married Minnie McGiven in 1898. They had one daughter, Artella Mae 'Artie.' Minnie passed away in 1905. Gene asked his brother, William, and Williams wife, Mary, to care for his five-year old daughter, Artie. He remarries Addie Kelley in 1907, and they raise a daughter, Alice Elizabeth and a son, Tracy. Both Tracy B., less than a year old, and his mother, Addie, passed away in 1911. Gene relocated to Stockton Springs where he worked as a carpenter at a shipyard. His third marriage was to Lydia J. Williams who was originally from Wellington. They returned to Bingham, where he resumed his carpentry business of repairing houses. Lydia passed away in 1940. Alone again, he kept himself busy as a saw filer. At the age of 86, David Eugene Powell passed away in 1961. He is buried in the Caratunk Village Cemetery.

James Edwin "Ed" Powell, named after his father and deceased infant brother, was born in 1876. Living in Madison, he married Florence Maude Pierce in 1898. They moved in with her family in Anson. He was a day laborer on a farm and later became the manager at a lumber camp. He and Florence had one son, Ernest S., born in 1899. Later in 1919, Ed and his brother, Tracy, worked in the woods at Rockwood for Stoddard of Bingham. In 1921, he worked in Greenville for the American Shoe Findings Company. By 1930, he and his family lived in Bingham where he was foreman at the Shank factory. He relocated to Skowhegan where he worked as a millwright, and became the maintenance man at the woolen mill. At the age of 85, James Edwin Powell passed away in Skowhegan in 1961. Florence passed away in 1962. They are both buried at the Village Cemetery in Bingham.

Evelyn (Eva, Evie) Stewart Powell was born in 1879. She married John Redmond, a farmer from Bingham, in 1902. They raised two daughters: Jessie Wilson who was born in 1903, and Mary Joyce who was born in 1906. John was a teamster in the lumbering industry. In 1930, Jesse married Raymond Hunnewell. They, along with their son, Stanton, moved in with John and Eva in Bingham. By 1940, John and Eva are divorced. Eva moved to Skowhegan to live with her second daughter, Mary, and Mary's husband, Howard Stuart. John, Jessie, and her family continued to live in Bingham. John Redmond passed away in 1948 and is buried in Bingham. Eva passed away at the age of ninety-one in 1971. She is buried next to her sister, Mary Elizabeth, in the Webster Cemetery in Caratunk.

William H. was born June 1881. He married Mary Kelley in 1903. William and Mary had no children of their own but raised brother Eugene's and Minnie's daughter Artella. In 1910, they lived in Caratunk, where William worked as a laborer doing odd jobs. By 1918, he was logging for himself before becoming a lumber camp cook. He and Mary then lived in Moxie Gore at William H. King's lumber camp. They had returned to Caratunk by 1926. I could not find any further records of them until I discovered William as Skowhegan's Chief of Police in the 1950's census. Mary passed away in 1955 and William in 1966. They are buried in the Bingham Village Cemetery.

Agnes A. Powell was born May 1884. She married John F. Durgin, a lumberman, in 1904. On June 28, 1905 their child was stillborn, and Agnes passed away the next day from heart failure. She was just twenty-one. Agnes is buried in the Durgin Cemetery.

Alfred Allen Powell was born May, 1888. He was a veteran of WWI. In the 1910 Census he was listed as a teamster in the lumbering business. In the 1920 Census he was listed as a farmer in The Forks and still lived with his father. He married Lois M. Piper in 1921. Lois was twenty-five and was born in Ione, California. She and Alfred moved to Hampden, Maine where Alfred was a fireman at a hotel. They had one son, Louis Maynard, born around 1922. Alfred and Lois divorced. She and their son relocated to Monson. Alfred returned to Caratunk. In 1935, he married Ada Martin Clowater, who had moved back to Maine from Canada. Later, Ada's daughter, Ruby E. Clowater, joined them. By 1950, Alfred, once a teamster, became a part-time U.S. postal mail carrier. Ada passed away in 1952 at the age of 69 and is buried in the Village Cemetery in Caratunk. Alfred remarried Elizabeth Hanscom McKenzie in 1955. Alfred Powell passed away in 1962 and is buried in the Village Cemetery, Caratunk. Elizabeth passed away in 1973 and is buried in the Whitefield Cemetery.

The ninth child, Winfield Scott, was born November 1893. In 1915, he married Edna Iola Pushor. He was employed by Dead River Log Driving Co., Dead River. He and Edna divorced in 1918. He was in the U.S. Army, 301st Amm. Train, Co G, 76 Division. From May 1918 to July 1919, he served in World War I as a cook. He returned to The Forks Plantation where his widowed father lived. He continued his cooking profession at lumber camps, and with years of experience, was employed as a professional cook at the Pleasant Pond Hotel.

[The hotel first opened in 1894, and later,
became known as the Pleasant Pond Inn.]

In 1920, he married Mabel Turner and moved to Palermo, where he worked for the next thirty years in a shingle mill. They had no children. In 1950, he registered as a farmer and owned his own farm. Winfield suffered from pulmonary emphysema and chronic bronchitis for 8 years. Mabel had passed away in 1961. Winfield made his home with his brother, William, in 1964 and passed away in 1965. Winfield Scott is buried in the Hannan Cemetery in Palermo.

Twins, Alta Mildred and Avis Estelle, were born May 1896. Alta married Guy M. Beane on October 11, 1913. They had three children: Lena M., born in 1914; Gladys L., born in 1916; and Lizzie B.; born in 1919. Lizzie lived only four days. Alta passed away in Portland in February 1963. Guy passed away in 1967. Alta, Guy, and daughter Lizzie are buried at the Moscow Union Cemetery.

Avis married Morris Ralph Martin, a lumberman from Caratunk, on August 30, 1913. [His parents were Terrance and Effie Martin. Morris was one of sixteen children.] They had ten children: Bernard, Ervin, Agnes, Hazel, Orrin, Glenis, Wesley, Helen, Leslie, Merline. An Eleventh child, David, was adopted. Merline lived to be only two years old. Avis moved to Richmond with seven of her children sometime between 1935 and 1940. I have found no record of Morris Martin from the 1930 census until his death in Caratunk in August of 1959. Avis passed away in August 1963, just six months after her twin sister Alta. Both Avis and Morris are buried in the Moscow Union Cemetery, as is her twin Alta.

The Sizeland Farm

The last farmer who moved from Hangtown was William E. Sizeland. Although the farm stayed in the family for years afterward, it seems that none of the children or grandchildren chose to live there.

Sizeland's oldest, daughter, Florence May, was born in June 1891. She became a school teacher and occasionally taught at the Hangtown School. By 1910, she was a high school teacher and living at Hangtown. On February 10, 1912, she married Casper Cook. They moved to Lewiston, and later relocated to Auburn. Their daughter, Irene S, was born in 1916. Casper worked in the Shoe Shop as McKay Sewer. In 1930, he was a retail merchant in a grocery store. He moved on to be a salesman, and by 1950, he was a manager of a grocery store. Florence May passed away in 1975. Casper R. Cook passed on in 1977. They are buried in the Mount Auburn Cemetery. Their daughters, Irene S., and her husband, Elmore K. Putnam; and Olive F., and her husband, Donald O. Skinner, are also buried there.

William "Henry" E. Sizeland, was born May 31, 1892 at The Forks. At age eighteen he was a teamster and lumbering like many others his age. After serving six months overseas, in 1919, Henry married Ann Celia Ledger. They lived in Auburn and worked at the shoe factory. By 1930, they have two sons, Earl, age 7, and Elwin, age 5. Henry continued working in the shoe factory per the 1950 census. William and Celia died the same year, 1969. They are buried at Mount Hope Cemetery, Lewiston. Their two sons and their wives are buried there as well.

Velma M. was born February 17, 1898. She, too, attended the Washington school and later was a school teacher there in 1916. She married a divorcee, Parker W. Otis, from Carmel, in 1919 and moved to Moscow. Parker was a telephone operator for the railroad station. Velma was a schoolteacher. Their first child was stillborn on May 19, 1920. Their second child, Louise Mary, was born on July 23, 1921. Velma continued her teaching career. In 1930, they lived in Bingham, and Parker was a station agent for the Railroad Stream. Another daughter, Marion S., was born in 1924 and Velma's father, William, lived with them. By 1940, they lived in Wales, Maine. William had passed away, and Parker was a telegraph operator. Velma dedicated two decades to her role as the U.S. Postmaster in Leeds Junction—1941-1961—finally retiring at sixty-three. Parker Otis died June 2, 1957 at the age of seventy, and Velma died Jun 1, 1975 in Augusta, age seventy-seven. They are buried at the Highland Cemetery in Carmel.

As previously mentioned, the Sizeland property stayed in the family until 1986 when it, too, followed the demise of the other Hangtown farms and was bought by a logging company.

CHAPTER 22

HANGTOWN REBORN

THE BEGINNING OF the breakdown of The 100 Acres— Formerly: Spaulding, Clark, Martin-1879, Prince-1895, Sizeland-1898 and now A.S. & C.B. Gould-1986.

After purchasing Sizeland's farm and land in 1986, A.S. & C.B. Gould & Sons, a logging company from Cornville, harvested a mix of hardwood and softwood from it. The 100 Acres was divided by the Hangtown Road, with roughly 60.0 acres on the east side and 40 acres on the west side. In 1987, Gould conveyed 2.686 acres on the west side to Michael R. Sackett and Jack K. Brake, surveyors and avid hunters from Skowhegan.

The following year, Gould sold the remaining 37.31 acres on the west side to Mark G. Kahler, Sackett and Brake's friend and hunting buddy. Goulds & Sons sold the last of its holdings, 60 acres on the east side of the Hangtown Road, to Sackett & Brake Survey, Inc. in 1989. Goulds & Sons" were no longer owners of land in Hangtown. Later Sackett & Brake conveyed the land holdings in Hangtown to their individual equities. They held this 60 acres for four years, then in 1994, they decided to sell 6.06 acres to Frederic P. Curran of Littleton,

Massachusetts, along with the condition of "no further division". Curran built a twenty foot by twenty-four-foot camp with a twelve-foot deck. Soon after, he had a neighbor.

In May of 1995, Larry Fuller of Canaan, Maine bought 8.0 acres on the east side of the Hangtown Road from Sackett and Brake with the condition—no further division. Fuller proceeded to build a seasonal camp, twenty-eight by thirty-two feet, with a closed-in loft at one end.

Keeping their 2.686 acres on the west side of the Hangtown Road, Sackett and Brake sold the remaining east side acreage to Fuller with 24.02 acres and Curran with 24.02 acres in the year 2000. At this time, they released the condition of —no further development referenced in the previous conveyances.

Nearly ten years of hunting, four wheeling, and snowmobiling passed before Fuller in 2004 sectioned out 1.0 acre of land from his original 8.0 acres. He built a trappers cabin to rent and accepted the offer to buy Sackett and Brake's remaining holdings in Hangtown, the 2.686 acres. As it turned out, in December he sold the newly built trapper's cabin along with 1.0 acre to Christopher Doughty from Cumberland. A few months later, in February 2005, Fuller sold his first camp and 7.0 acres along with the 24.02 acres to Andy Coone from Dyer's Road, Moxie Gore. Coone was the first farmer and homesteader in Hangtown since 1929.

Curran was busy building as well. He built a smaller camp to the north of the first. In 2005, before he sold his first camp, he moved the new one further east on his property. He offered Fuller the purchase of the 5.513 acres the camp had been sitting on. Fuller was already building his third camp on his own west side property. In December 2006, Michael and Carol Macaulay from Seven Hundred Acre Island bought Fuller's third camp situated on the 2.686 acres on the west side of the Hangtown Road, along with his 5.513 acres on the east side. This leaves Fuller without land in Hangtown—but not for long.

Curran did sell his original camp with 4.83 acres to Michael and

Carolee DeRoche of Benton in 2006. Living in his small camp situated on his northeast border, Curran decided to hire Fuller and his son to build a larger camp for him in 2007. The small old camp was dragged out of the way and the building began.

Mark Kahler's land in Hangtown has been idle since 1988. He had camped on his property, off and on, while he tested products for L.L.Bean, but had not built on it. In August 2007, Kahler decided to sell his property to Fuller. Fuller decided to section out 10.0 acres and sell the remaining 27.31 acres to the Macaulay's, whose land abutted it. The Macaulay's counter-offered and purchased the total 37.31 west side acres and sold their east side parcel of 5.513 acres to Fuller in 2008. Fuller built his fourth camp in Hangtown in 2009.

In 2012, Curran decided to section out 3.59 acres, moved his old small camp onto it, and sold it to Earl and Stephanie Varney of Turner.

Curran decided he would rather be on the water than in the woods, and sold his remaining property, 16.355 acres, including the camp and buildings, to Joanne Gurney of Benton in 2012. This also included an easement of access from Bayroot, LLC which Curran had obtained. The easement gave him a right of way from the intersection of the Hangtown Road onto the Crossover Road, and to cross land owned by Bayroot which allowed Curran a driveway to his camp. In 2019, Gurney transferred ownership of her property to her daughter, Susan, and son-in-law, Doug Blaisdell. They sold to Eric and Beth Glidden of South Berwick in 2020.

All this time Andy Coone had been homesteading for nine years and he decided to make some changes of his own. He built a smaller camp on his property further back from the road and to the south. In 2014, he sold 3.0 acres and his old camp, Fuller's first camp, with all buildings to Carol Macaulay and Larry Fuller, Sr. of Lincolnville. In 2015, they sold it to Fuller's son, Jr. of Solon, only to buy it back in 2018. Known as #1 camp, Macaulay and Fuller sold it to Craig Farrington from Hebron and Scott Farrington from Minot in 2019.

After Andy Coone's passing in 2020, his estate sold the 28.0 acres including buildings, to Carol Macaulay from Hangtown, The Forks Plantation, in 2021.

Christopher Doughty who had owned his camp, Fuller's #2 The Trapper's Camp, for nineteen years, sold it to Fuller and Macaulay, from Hangtown, The Forks Plantation, in 2023. They almost immediately sold it to Randy and Jonah Farrington of Minot.

Summary of the owners today of the 100acres, Lot #21, Hangtown, Maine

Eric and Beth Glidden 16.355a

Matt and Leah Alexander 3.59a

Mike and Carolee DeRoche 4.83a

Larry Fuller Sr. 5.513a

Carol Macaulay 68.116a

Craig and Scott Farrington 3.0a

Randy and Jonah Farrington 1.0a

All is quiet in this section of Hangtown, as observed by the only homesteaders left. It gets a little busy during hunting season, ice fishing, and snowmobiling, though. However, not as busy as it was one night in 2009.

CHAPTER 23

THE WOODS ARE NOT ALWAYS SERENE

The following stories are based on true events, with certain names changed and details enhanced for narrative effect.

Fire at the Hangtown Intersection

It was a cold, damp late afternoon in May, 2009. With the sun just barely visible behind the evergreen trees that blocked the view of Sugarloaf and the Bigalows, Larry Fuller and his son were on their way home from the construction site of Larry's new camp, #4. With the pickup truck hauling a trailer full of lumber to be returned, Larry was picking his way through the muddy ruts—so obvious on these wood's roads in early spring. Not expecting traffic on this seldom-used, one-lane road, they swerved to avoid an oncoming, newer-model car just as it whizzed by them. Larry caught a glimpse of a man and women who were seemingly engrossed in exuberant conversation, their arms flailing and mouths were spread wide with hysterical laughter. They seemed not to comprehend their near collision with his now mired truck and trailer. Without hesitation the car continued on towards the intersection of the Crossover road and the Hangtown road.

Not recognizing the car nor the inhabitants, as Larry and his son worked feverously to free the mud-mired truck from the ditch, they wondered who this couple was and where they were headed. It seemed unlikely for this newer car to be on a woods road, and Larry questioned if they indeed knew where they were going. The Crossover Road ends as it comes to the seemingly forever muddy Hangtown Road. Knowing that Fred Curran was at his camp at Hangtown, the guys assumed the cock-a-hoop couple must be headed for Fred's. With more important things to do at present, Larry decided to check with Fred in the morning when cell phone service should be better. But then again, it could be worse.

Cell phone service is limited in the Hangtown area. There is no land line service along with no electrical power. The area is totally off the grid! To make things even more difficult, the cell service is limited to very few spots where one can connect. Cell phone boosters are effective, but they require power, which can be provided by generators or by plugging into DC power source, such as your vehicle. Even then the service can be limited and/or intermittent.

After filling and backing, the truck finally spun out of the ditch and onto the solid but slimy road. Larry hesitated, wondering if he should follow the couple, but with his load and the sun now setting behind the Bigalows, it was best for him to continue on and get home before dark.

It was around mid-night when Fred Curran was awakened by a loud explosion. Somewhat confused by what sounded like a cannon blast, he opened his cabin door to loud yelling. His first assumption was that someone was partying. Another boom and someone hollering for help hastened him to quickly close the door, get dressed, and search out what was causing all the commotion. As a precaution he retrieved his pistol and loaded it. Now, fully awake it donned on him to try calling his girlfriend who, upon reaching her, strongly advised him to stay put and call the sheriff.

Fred did call 911, the Madison Sheriff responded, and Fred gave him directions to get to Hangtown. At this time of year the old Hangtown road was impassable and one needed to use Bayroot's Boise road and Crossover road. Fred waited by his DC-boosted cell phone for the sheriff in case he got lost. It was a good thing, since the sheriff missed the turn, ended up on the dead-end Preacher's Road, and needed further directions. Fred told him to turn around, take a right at the end of the Preacher's Road onto Boise Road, head south, and then take his next right. A half-hour later, another explosion sent Fred scurrying to the window, just as the sheriff drove-in. Fred jumped in with the sheriff, and together they proceeded down Crossover road. As they reached the Hangtown intersection, they saw a car in the triangle of the intersection, fully engulfed in bright yellow and white flames, with black smoke tumbling upward to the night sky. To their left, sat two people, appearing to be in their mid-seventies, on the tailgate of Andy Coone's pickup truck. They were both wrapped in a small piece of plastic, which somewhat sheltered them from the rain. (Andy owned the homestead further north on the Hangtown road. Not able to manage driving through the mud this time of year, he always parked near the intersection. A rather scantily dressed man, sporting shorts and a bandage around his torso, sat beside a woman in what once were white shorts and a pink t-shirt. Both seemed hypothermic. The sheriff quickly put the two in his vehicle, complimented Fred on his quick thinking and assistance, and sped off. By now, the car had completely burned and was no longer considered a danger, except for obstructing a now larger mud hole on the Hangtown road.

The sheriff had arranged for the car to be dragged out that night, and by the next day all that remained of the incident was a bit of debris and remnants of an obvious vehicle fire.

Larry called Fred the next morning asking about the couple who had driven him off the road the day before. A somewhat groggy Fred filled him in on the previous night's episode. Later, when Larry arrived in Hangtown the two spent hours discussing how the car might have caught on fire. They concurred that the couple, seemingly on a joy ride, got stuck in the mud and didn't know any better than to keep spinning their mud-mired tires, causing overheating and eventually the fire.

It was not long before the two reminisced and shared events of other Hangtown episodes.

The Search for Two Brothers

It was in 1994 when a search went out for two brothers who had attacked and beaten a man earlier that day. They had recently been released from jail and had violated probation and were thought to be in the Hangtown area. The sheriff, deputies, and others were searching the area when they came onto Greg's camp.

Roused from a stolen after-lunch nap, Greg—a new resident on the Hangtown Road—awoke to the banging on his front door. Rather alarmed at the site of an officer and two deputies on his doorstep, Greg, with great apprehension hesitantly opened his door. The County Sheriff introduced himself and his deputies before relating the reason for the intrusion. He informed Greg of the situation at hand with concluding that they suspected the violators were in the vicinity of Hangtown. Somewhat relieved that the visit did not otherwise involve him, Greg related how he had seen no one around for days. He agreed to stay vigilant and report any sightings to the officials. Little did the sheriff realize that electronic communication was pretty much nil in this area.

Left to himself, Greg locked his doors and windows, pulled the curtains until just a slit enabled him to peek out through. He hoped that they would find the suspects soon and once again he could resume his daily routine. However, the search continued into the evening when he heard the rhythmic thwop-thwop-thwop of a helicopter. Opening the door for a better look, he found himself flooded in extreme brightness as the searchlight of the helicopter swept over the area. He wondered if they had a Dual-Mode searchlight giving them the FLIR thermal imaging along with enhanced visibility or IR LED light source. Only Greg would think of this. It was a strange, eerie sight watching the helicopter sweeping the dense and usually serene woods. The helicopter made multiple trips circling over roughly 400 acres until sometime around midnight Greg could hear them no more. It seemed the search must be over.

He was again surprised with a knocking on his door so late at night. Greg lifted the corner of the curtain to find, for the second time that day, the sheriff on his doorstep. Opening the door, Greg glanced around for the deputies while the sheriff explained that everyone had gone home. Apologizing for his late night visit, the sheriff gave a rendition of the exhausted search for the two "convicts". Hikers on the AT were quite certain they had seen the suspects earlier in the day heading west on the trail. With this information, the search had moved closer to Route 201, which would have presented a faster means of escape for the suspects. Having brought Greg up to speed with the latest developments, the sheriff bid him goodnight and left in the County Sheriff pickup truck. Finally, peace was returned to Hangtown.

After all the commotion, Greg was finally able to relax. He mixed himself a night toddy and lit up a smoke, trying not to think about whether the two convicts were still around Hangtown, or if, indeed, they had hiked off to faster lanes. Suddenly alarmed by a gust of wind rattling the window, he hesitated with his pull, saying aloud, "Uh, maybe two drinks"!

A Ghost Jeep at Holly Brook

Under the cover of darkness, two vehicles quietly made their way along the rough old Hangtown Road. The first being a jeep driven by a perturbed individual who had decided to relocate a rival's jeep. Whether it was planned or accidental, the jeep went off the bridge and into the running water of Holly Brook balancing on its side as the

Brook swiftly flowed through. If the driver got wet, will probably never be known. Was the second vehicle to pick up the driver? Probably but still a mystery!

❧

Nearby, stumbling over the fallen pine tree with its branches brushing his sweaty face, thinking, 'what's another little pitch going to matter', Pete stepped off the Appalachian Trail into the middle of the Hangtown Road. He had read in one of the journals which was left by another hiker, Andy Coone, that the Trail passed close to Holly Brook. Nearly exhausted, dirty, and fighting off the blackflies for days, the brook seemed to be just the refuge he was looking for. Gathering what energy he had, he left the Trail and hiked the few yards south to the brook.

The brook running east to west was spanned by an old low bridge. Pete decided to slide down the bank on the west side of the bridge where he spotted a flat rock to sit on. Removing his ragged boots and stiff, odiferous socks, he plunged his tired feet into the icy water. Regardless of the cold, he kept them submerged feeling the swelling in his feet and ankles gradually diminish. It had been a long hard walk and he had not stopped for days while trying to catch up with two other hikers called The Rafters. Looking through leaved out limbs of a fallen maple, he thought he could see the underside of a vehicle in the brook. The image reminded him of the horse he had recently seen in one farmer's pasture. The horse was lying on its side with hooves sticking outwards, and quite dead. Shaking that image off, Pete looked around and seeing no one near, called out, but no one responded. Figuring the owners had left for help, he replaced his footwear and crawled up the bank deciding to set up camp in a clearing he had spotted back near the trail. It was late and he had no interest in heating up any food. Snacking on a protein bar, he set up his tent, crawled in, and, for better words, passed out.

❧

Early that next morning found one of Hangtown's camp owners parked on the Holly Brook Bridge surveying the scene of what appeared to be an accident. Close, and to the east of the bridge, was a jeep nearly rolled on its side, awash in the brook. Just then three bicyclist came wheeling down the hill on a collision course with the camp owner's truck. A near pile-up as the three cyclists simultaneously braked becoming google-eyed at the scene of the jeep wallowing in the brook.

As to who called the sheriff is unclear and by the time he arrived another camp owner was scrutinizing the scene as well. Arriving the same time as the sheriff, was a tow truck. The driver set to work hooking up to the rear bumper of the jeep. It did not take long before the jeep was on dry, solid ground again. Still hooked up to the tow truck, slowly and in a single file, the truck, the dripping jeep, and the sheriff pulling up the rear, slowly filed up over Holly Brook Hill and out of Hangtown.

It was noted that the sheriff seemed little concerned with the obvious leakage of gasoline in Holly Brook.

The excitement on the Old Hangtown Road and Holly Brook Bridge dwindled as the observing parties gathered their own vehicles and further cleared the scene.

The buzzing of mosquitoes trying to enter the tent awoke Pete late in the morning. He lay in his tent savoring the protection from the mosquitoes and, yes, those obnoxious blackflies. Drifting back to sleep, it was the growling of his stomach that next awoke him. Starving, he rolled out of his bag contemplating on prepping a big meal. Having missed the breakfast hour he decided on cooking some of those fresh vegetables he procured from the Hiker's Box at the Caratunk post office. He salivated thinking of his dried soup mix supplemented with those fresh vegetables and complimented with much needed coffee! Having forgotten to fill his water bottles the night before, he headed to the brook to fill it. Groggy . . . his mind snapped to attention remembering seeing the vehicle in the brook the night before. 'Just how good would that water be', he thought. When he reached the brook, however, there was no vehicle in sight. Scratching his head, he mentally questioned – 'how beat was I last night?' He was sure he had seen a vehicle on its side in the fast flowing brook. He had not heard any noises during the night. Could he have imagined the whole thing being as tired as he had been? 'Was it a mirage or did I really see it', he wondered. He could only conclude that the trail was getting to him; best to get going before he completely lost his mind.

Pitter-Patter On Their Roof—No, not rain, sleet or ice.

Having left home early that morning it seemed forever before they were finally out of the unusually heavy traffic. Approaching Caratunk, they chose the first exit off 201. They proceeded into the town recognizing what used to be the old store, now only harboring the Caratunk post office and offering room and apartment rentals. Turning right onto the Pleasant Pond Road, it would be only three miles before they would take a left turn onto the old Hangtown Road. Remembering how rough and narrow the road was when on their last visit, they opened a celebratory beer for the trip in. They had another two and a half miles to go on an old woods road-better described as a horse path! Cupping their beer and allowing it to swing like a ship's gimbal, one tire then another dropped into crevices of the unforgiving ledge lying smack in the middle of the road. There was no way to avoid these obstacles. One took chances driving on the Hangtown Road, which harbored deep mud, crushed and sharp exposed surfaces of metal culverts, and boulders in want of gravel to hide under. The scenery was pleasant enough, nicely forested, with plenty of partridge, in the path. The birds, alert with outstretched necks, prepared to take flight as the rare appearance of the vehicle made its way across their paths.

Slowing the vehicle, the travelers weaved through the pine forest, down over Holly Brook Hill, approaching the brook and the old, nearly collapsed bridge. They both took a pull of their beer contemplating that they may finally have use for the DC powered winch which her mother had given them two years ago .

The bridge crossing went smoothly, followed with spinning and catching ground as they drove up over more loose rocks. Just shy of the top of the hill, they met with another mutilated steel culvert where they, in fear of cutting their tires, pulled right scraping the side of the new truck with limbs.

Finally they broke out of the woods with an old logging yard on their left and on their right was the Crossover road. They were not that familiar with the Crossover road but they were aware further on that road was another woods road to the left. This is what was called the Loop road. Up in this country people were quite loose with their definition of roads!

The travelers remembered they could head south from their camp on the Hangtown road, and take a left onto the Crossover road. The next left is the Loop road and that road leads around to intersect with the north end of the Hangtown road- mostly hidden by undergrowth. Doing this would bring them right back to their doorstep. It was a nice walk. Just once they drove through, ultimately spending hours buffing out the scratches on his new green Ford pickup truck.

It was not far now into camp. Their beer almost consumed, they concentrated on watching for the two camps coming up on their right, wondering if anyone was in. The first driveway showed no occupancy, no tracks leading in, and no vehicle. They could see very little of the camp somewhat hidden by trees and the curve of the driveway. There were wheel tracks leading to the next camp which was sitting high and far back from the road. Seeing no smoke coming from the chimney, and no vehicle in sight it seemed this one was vacant, as well.

Around the next turn was their camp, not far off the road at all. The log sided cabin was just what they had always pictured as a get-a-way for them. The bonus was the view. Around back was a small field showing stumps where big trees had been. The previous owner had cut them, producing logs which he sawed into lumber, and used it to build the cabin. It was not the stumps that grabbed their attention. It was the incredible sight of Sugarloaf and the Bigelows stretching skyward and shadowing the other mountains and hills nearby. A magnificent view, and it was theirs!

Their two black, male dogs now awake and alert with the stopping of the truck, leaped out as the back door opened. First sniffing the fire pit they disappeared to find a tree to relieve themselves.

Opening the door to their one room cabin, the first thing she noticed was an empty beer can on the table. How strange, she always cleaned off the table, putting everything away especially any sign of alcohol which might tempt someone to break in. Ignoring it for now, she hurriedly started her chores. First was building a much needed fire in the woodstove as her husband went to fetch buckets of water from the nearby covered spring. After retrieving more firewood from the woodshed, the groceries were collected from the back body of the truck. Placing perishables in the refrigerator she frowned thinking she was sure she had left beer in the bottom vegetable drawer. Once the groceries were stowed, they mixed drinks and settled at the butcher block table, taking in the sweet smell of new wood and the serenity of the cabin.

With a smile on her face, she scanned their one-room cabin. As she sat facing the front door, to its right was their queen-size bed, covered with the homemade patchwork quilt her mother had made for her so many years ago. A picture of her mother sat on the campy bureau between the bed and the gas refrigerator. There wasn't much unused space in the cabin. Next to the refrigerator was a small apartment style gas stove with a bit of counter between. More counter space continued with small, homemade overhead pine cabinets. A double stainless steel sink with a window above it allowed her to look through to the enclosed porch and out through its window, offering views of the mountains. Along the other wall was a metal futon with a black mattress, a roughly made woodbox, and a woodstove sitting on a hearth made of cement and stone. Another window opened to the porch. At the last minute the builder decided to close in the porch to create more sitting or sleeping facilities.

As she reached for her drink, a piece of paper on the table caught her attention. It appeared to be a bill. Picking it up she wondered how this propane bill had found its way onto their table. The date confirmed that it had not been there when she had previously left. How suspicious it was to be on the table, and not tucked into the outside door as most vendors would do. Oh well, nothing to do about it now, but something that she felt needed to be addressed in the near future. This evening they would relax, watch the sun slide down behind the mountain range, and do some reading which they seldom have time in their regular routine to do.

After a supper of seared deer steak and salad, they sat at the table watching Sugarloaf and the Bigelows recede into darkness. Then with the gas lights on over the table, they opened their books settling in for a few hours of reading. How nice it seemed to be able to sit quietly- no phones, no TV, only their two labs snoring as they lay on their L.L. Bean beds.

Fully engrossed with what they were reading, a low growl caught their attention. Thinking it must be just the anxiety of new surroundings, she hushed her lab and returned to her book. Another low growl, from both dogs this time, brought her to her feet. Now fully alert and listening intently, she could hear the distant report of a gun. It was hunting season after all but it was dark and well after shooting hours. She stood listening as another closer shot rang out. Frowning, she looked at her husband, who, with reading glasses half-way down his nose and one hand flat on his opened book, looked up at her questioningly. About then they could hear a vehicle coming. They could not fathom what was happening. Just then another shot, closer, with pitter-patter on the roof. No sir, that was not rain, sleet or ice. That was pellets bouncing and tumbling. Still standing at the table and not quite knowing what to do, they quickly flipped off the gas lights. Now they could see the lights of the oncoming vehicle. The next shot is when she dives beside the wooden framed bed only inches off the floor. Her husband follows right behind her. The deafening barking and growling from the dogs continued with their hackles risen like bristles on a brush. Noses just inches from the cabin door, their barks continued as the truck eerily quiet, slowed and crept by the cabin. With no more shots heard, the couple slowly crawled from their cover, while wrestling with the dogs to gain access to the window. They peered through the darkness, straining to catch any telltale lights or lingering movements. The dogs once again hushed were still anxious to investigate the disturbance and wanted out. That was not going to happen. They were sent back to their respective beds and were consoled with milk bones.

Sighing with relief, at least for the moment, the couple mixed a nightcap and apprehensively sat at the table sipping their sedative. So much for tranquility at the cabin. This was not the quiet retreat they thought they had bought! It was a long night, waiting for dawn and harboring the anxiety of the vehicle's unwanted return! They hoped it had continued around the loop and out through the Crossover road to Boise road and Moxie, or wherever!

A call from their friend and neighbor the following morning shed some light on the previous night's episode. After hearing the story and being surprised at the occurrence, he surmised it was probably the occupants of the camp further north on the road. He confirmed that he would give them a call to verify it was them. Aware that they had possibly overreacted the night before, they assured him that they were not complaining and wanted no hard feelings with the neighbors.

Within an hour there was a non-obtrusive knock on their door. She turned away from the sink full of dishes, as her husband opened the door. There stood a man dressed in a green wool jacket, with his hands in his pockets and seemingly quite embarrassed. After introducing himself and with a cordial handshake, he promptly apologized for his rowdy behavior the night before. Accepting the apology, they invited him in for a cup of coffee. A new friendship was launched.

As she sipped yet another cup of coffee, she mentally reviewed the earlier conversation.

It appeared that he and his buddies had experienced a hard day of bird hunting in Jackman and were celebrating on their return to camp. They had not considered that other camp owners were in Hangtown. There was no mention of the number of birds they harvested.

Oh and what about the empty beer can on the table?

Ah yes, the question of the beer can and bill on the table. Their neighbor also relayed how the propane delivery man often used his credit card to enter customers' camps. He would then help himself to any available beer while sitting at their table, writing the bill and leaving it there.

She figured it was his idea of free beer while saving postage!

Bang, Bang

Some years ago when Hangtown was relatively unoccupied it was not only used as a dumping area for household trash but also attracted individuals either hunting or testing their weaponry and accuracy. Calibers might range from a mere BB gun (ha) to a much higher powered gun. Regardless, there are always those who like to "practice". Some slightly energetic marksmen use the orange paper targets, some love the sound of those metal swinging targets, and the more adventurists search for a more engaging, rewarding mark.

Committed to completing this section of the Appalachian Trail, Hedgehog Bob pushed through the underbrush and climbed over fallen logs, making his way north to Monson and eventually to Mt. Katahdin. All was quiet after he left the truck traffic on Route 201 behind. He had picked up his supply package from the Caratunk post office late yesterday and spent the night at the Sterling Inn a few miles south of the AT on 201. After a good breakfast and a ride back to the Trail, he was once again cursing the blackflies, yet enjoying the sight of chickadees flitting from branch to branch. Fantasizing that they were eating more than their weight in blackflies encouraged him to keep trekking.

The stillness was suddenly broken by the rat-a-tat-tat of what was obviously not the pileated woodpecker. He had heard it hammering earlier as it fed on carpenter ants from the old rotten tree. No, this was gunshots, a series of them, causing him to freeze in place while looking about for some sort of cover. His first thought was that it must be hunters but then he realized that the seasons were closed for hunting. Not only that, but he thought, if the target was being hunted for meat, with all those bullets there would be nothing left of it. He yelled out, hoping to bring attention to whomever was shooting that he was nearby. Not knowing where they were or the direction they were shooting in, he flattened himself on the wet pine needles covering the forest floor. For more than half-an-hour he kept low; yelling out each time the barrage of bullets ceased, until he finally heard vehicles departing south. Full of apprehension Hedgehog Bob proceeded to, and crossed, the Hangtown road; losing himself in the tumbled down forest and away from this dubious civilization.

Just before dark, a camp owner driving by the old log field noticed a vehicle nestled against the tree line. First thinking someone was lost or in trouble, he stopped his truck, and ventured closer on foot only to find the car had been riddled with bullets, and a lot of bullets. There were empty cartridges left all over the ground there. He hesitated, looked around, and then cautiously strode towards the vehicle to investigate further. The fear of finding a body slowed his pace and hastened his heartbeat. To his great relief, there was no bloody body, no one, and nothing in the old, and abandoned car. Slowly letting out his breath, he realized the car had been a prop for target practice. He wanted to know who was responsible for this untidy invasion of the forest and if they were going to clean up the mess.

Other camp owners, hikers, sightseers were curious and irritated as well with the bullet-riddled car and debris scattered around it. Questions were asked but no one seemed to take responsibility-until one evening. Seemingly thought to be a joke, the riddled car some-how found its way to the front steps of one of the camps. Needless to say, that camp owner was vexed at such a deposit on his property. Approaching the point of anger, he made it known to the suspect party that he wanted it 'off his property.' Not much of a row evolved, and by the next day, the riddled car had vanished. Where it was ultimately abandoned remains a mystery for the Hangtown historian. But this was far from the end of the pranks.

CHAPTER 24

CAMPS AND PRANKS

There are many reasons for going to camp.

You have the serious fisherman, hunters, and snowmobilers.

There are jollies with fistfuls of beer, whiskey glasses and ice teas.

The serious knitters, readers, and writers.

The ambitious hikers, climbers—and sleepers?

Camp fires, hot dogs and marshmallows,

The fish fries, pig roasts, and—Pranksters!

Welcome to camp

It was exciting to be invited to camp. Immediately, Molly had imagined a quaint cottage on the edge of a lake, or maybe pond. She would take her bright orange kayak to paddle evenings, watching the sunset—mornings, she would listen to the loons as she drowsily lay in bed waiting for the smell of coffee.

Just how many miles was it off the main highway, she wondered, as one front tire once again dropped into a hole in the dusty gravel road. 'Woods road,' they had said—she thinking they meant the name of the street or lane. She could now see what was meant by woods road. There were trees leaning over the road from both sides. Once she had to nearly drive into the ditch to avoid the huge branches of one that had fallen into the path of her Mazda CX-3. Having turned left onto another dirt road, she glanced at the hastily written directions that said to take the next right.

At the next right, she turned, driving until she came to alder trees on both sides, drooping over what was no bigger than a four-wheeler path. Obviously, she had mistakenly taken a wrong turn.

"But the note said next right," she muttered to herself. 'Oh well', she thought, 'I'll have to turn around.' Before doing that she had to relieve herself. She could hold it no longer!

Fighting those little black, biting flies she swiftly did her business and quickly returned to her car.

She drove on until she came up on top of a small hill. In front of her bloomed an amazing horizon filled with tall dark green mountain peaks- the sun barely visible between them.

A "T" in the road is where she must turn right and as she did she spotted a sign which read Hangtown Rd! "What have I got myself into?" She mumbled. But it was too late now to turn back. She did not want to be caught on any of those roads which she had just traveled after dark, and dark was coming on fast. Take the second driveway on the right she had been told.

Hesitantly, she continues up the long dirt driveway, realizing her lakeside dreams have been washed away with dust. And now, this woodsy cabin materializes in front of her. Knowing there was no way of backing out of her commitment to spend the weekend with an old college mate, she faked a smile and knocked on the door.

With just one glance, Anna realized, Molly had not fully under-stood where she had been invited. Molly stood in the doorway dressed in shorts, a blue t-shirt, and sandals. And with blackflies swarming around her head. Pausing to wave off the nasty annoying bugs, Molly gave Anna a quick hug before hastily pushing through the doorway with her Delsey luggage in tow.

Anna caught a sweet whiff of perfume-compared it to her deep-woods bug spray and knowingly smiled.

"I guess I had the wrong impression of camp," Molly smiled trying to hide her disappointment.

"You're going to love it," Anna said handing Molly a glass of home-made sangria.

"Oh, I know I will once I find something to ward off those flies," as she took a sip from her wine glass. "What is this anyway?" she blurted as the wine tickled her throat.

"Sangria, I make it myself from berries I picked this summer, then add some brandy, fruit, and something for fizz. One time, I couldn't find any soda so I added an Alka-Seltzer. Not good! After that, I bought a Soda Stream to make my own when I forget to bring some," she said, pausing to sip her drink. "You have to make do at camp," she continued, looking seriously over her glasses at her friend.

Daring not to shake her head at the whole idea, Molly sipped her wine as it began to taste better and better.

Soon the two were reminiscing about their college days, hardly noticing the darkness seeping through the windows.

After exhausting once forgotten but pleasant memories of college activities, the attention turned to more pressing matters.

"Let's have another glass of Sangria while we prepare dinner." Anna offered.

"Sounds like a plan." Molly replied while handing over her glass. "But first, where is the bathroom," she added.

"Number one or two," queried Anna.

"One," replied Molly, feeling like she was back in kindergarten.

"Around that corner to the left. It's a Porta-Potty. Just like the one we used on that boat when we fished with Joe. Hey, put the paper in the bag and we'll burn it later," Anna added smiling.

Molly found herself in a small closet bathroom. There was a shelf to her left, a paper bag under that, the porta-potty directly in front of her, and a shower stall with a faded curtain to her right.

"Phew," she thought, "at least there is a shower."

Peeking around the shower curtain she realized that it was not plumbed for water. An empty water bag hung over the shower rod. She had seen this type of bag before in the L.L. Bean catalog.

"I guess that's the shower," Molly mused as she returned to the kitchen, hesitating because she didn't know where to wash her hands.

"Right here," Anna coaxed pointing at the plastic jug with a little twist spout, which was balancing on the edge of the metal sink. As Molly washed her hands, Anna flipped the mooseburgers and reached for the salad from the propane refrigerator.

"Those smell yummy," Molly said as she felt her stomach rumble. "How long had it been since she had eaten last," she thought. She guessed it must have been that granola bar she found in her purse after leaving home that morning. She had meant to get up early, have breakfast and be out of the house by nine, but she had overslept. It had been ten before her cell phone awakened her.

"Are you on the road," Sam asked her.

"Huh, oh no," Molly said as she tumbled out of bed, nearly dropping the phone.

"Molly, it's almost ten and you said you were leaving early. What's with that?" Sam questioned as he fumbled with court papers on his desk.

"I, I know," she stuttered as she stumbled towards her bathroom door. "I'll call you back later; I've got to rush," she added as she reached for the faucet and cold water.

Forgetting about breakfast; once dressed and a quick application of make-up she grabbed her suitcase and purse, slamming her apartment door as she exited. She figured she could make up time by skipping lunch and pushing the speed limit! That granola bar had saved her!

∽

"It's mooseburger," Anna said as she looked slyly at her friend obviously interrupting Molly's thoughts.

Molly just stared wide-eyed and with nothing to say. And the burger smelled so good she convinced herself that it would be delicious. She wouldn't consider any other option. Placing the burgers on the table, they both dived in for the first bite. Molly was pleasantly surprised. It was delicious—no, it was more than delicious. It was better than the quarter pounder at McDonald's, which she thought was the best thing coming off a grill! She watched as Anna peeled off the top bun, added a bit of salad, and topped it off with a squirt of mayo before replacing the bun.

Hum, she thought, not a bad idea, as she mimicked Anna's actions.

With every bit of burger and salad consumed, the paper plates were shoved into the woodstove, and their third Sangria poured. Just as the gentleman in colonial times would retire to their den with snifters of cognac, they retired to the porch with their Red Cups of Sangria.

"Oh, don't sit in that chair," Anna spurted as she nearly spilled her drink.

Molly suddenly froze in her half-sitting position, wrestling with her Red Cup that she had squeezed so tightly pushing the Sangria nearly over the edge.

"Whaaat?" she exclaimed.

"Well Molly, I guess the best way to explain it is to show you," Anna announced as she rose from her wooden rocker, feeling a bit nervous with what she was about to expose, pondering what city-girl Molly's reaction would be.

As Anna sat in the subject chair, there was a loud fart. Molly's hand rushed to her mouth in embarrassment as uncontrollable laughter erupted from Anna. The laughter was contagious as Molly joined in, still not fully understanding what had just taken place.

"My husband is a prankster," Anna blurted out between guffaws of laughter. Why it struck her so funny she could not fathom. She had not found it amusing when he had played his prank on her. But now, seeing Molly's reaction she understood what she must have looked like when the joke was on her.

"But I don't see what's wrong with the chair," Molly innocently confessed. "What do you mean your husband is a prankster?"

Anna, realizing that Molly thought it was her all along, let out another wail of laughter. She stood up and abruptly sat down again releasing another loud fart. Molly stood there, eyebrows knitted in confusion, studying the situation. Anna once again rose and pointed to the contraption under the seat. He put this here so when someone sat down, there would be a loud fart, and everyone in the camp would stare at the victim of his prank.

A burst of nervous laughter came from Molly as she finally understood the prank. Once again seated in appropriate chairs, they silently stared into the darkness watching the June bugs perform their dance.

Molly, now tucked under her comforter for the night, relived the day's events in her mind. She had been uptight and disappointed with camp not being a cottage. She so wanted to swim and water ski, tube and kayak, lie in the warm summer breeze and get a tan to show off at work.

Oh, well, she thought, I'm here and need to make the best of it.

But seriously as the rudeness of the prankster's fart machine surfaced in her mind, she recalled how her first reaction was disgust. Now she found herself smiling at the volume of laughter it produced. It was good to let go with so much laughter, happy tears rolling down her face—sometimes finding their salty way onto her tongue. With that, she fell asleep with a smile on her face.

Her eyes popped open to darkness as she was suddenly awakened by some commotion above her bed. There was some sort of scuffle going on above the ceiling in her room. It sounded like something was racing, looping around and around. Then there was silence.

She heard Anna stirring in the next room.

"Anna," Molly called out. "What is going on—what am I hearing—it's a frightening noise."

"I don't know," Anna uttered sleepily. "I didn't hear anything."

"Something was racing around on my ceiling," Molly cried.

"Oh, that was probably our ermine hunting down mice in the attic," Anna threw out.

"Ermine, mice?" Molly nearly screamed.

"It's okay Molly," Anna soothed, "Ermines are no more than ferrets really, just wild. You don't have to feed them and they keep the mouse population down. He's probably gone already."

"Not soon enough," Molly barked.

"Go back to sleep," Anna mumbled with a big yawn, "It'll be daylight before you know it."

Molly pulled the comforter over her head knowing she would not be able to go back to sleep—really not wanting to—afraid she would have nightmares of ermines munching on mice, or maybe her!

She awoke to the smell of coffee and for a minute forgot where she was. Light was peeking around the homemade curtains that almost covered the windows. She tumbled out of her bed, said good morning to Anna as she stumbled towards the bathroom. Finding a wash cloth and towel beside a basin of warm water, she hastily washed. Returning to the kitchen she grabbed her Red Cup from last night, filled it, and stepped outside to brush her teeth.

A steaming cup of coffee awaited her on her return, along with a container of milk and sugar packets nestled next to it. Anna was already sipping her black coffee and teasingly smiling at Molly.

Molly looked up, frowned and queried, "What?"

"You should see yourself," Anna said nearly snorting her coffee.

"I could if you had a mirror in your bathroom," Molly retorted.

"You look like you have black eyes with all that make-up smudged like that," Anna chuckled in good humor. Here, check it out," as she passed over a small mirror to Molly.

"Oh geez," cried Molly when she saw her reflection. Then remembering, she continued, "Oh no, and I was in such a hurry yesterday—I know I forgot to pack my makeup."

"You won't need it here," Anna teased, "Ermines don't like it anyway."

"Then I should need it," Molly responded remembering last night's episode.

"You'll be alright," Anna said as she broke out in laughter, "I wish I could have seen your face when I told you what was making that noise."

"You wouldn't have been able to—I had that ragged sleeping bag pulled over my head!" Molly retorted in good humor, as she started giggling at the picture she must have presented.

"Time for breakfast," Anna declared as she rose from the counter stool and reached for the wooden cupboard door. "Pancakes?" she offered.

"Love them," replied Molly, adding, "Can I help?"

"Nah, I made some mix before I came up," said Anna.

"You make your own pancake mix?" Molly exclaimed, furrowing her eyebrows in disbelief once again.

"Sure and all I have to do is add milk, oil, and eggs. Oh no," Anna cried out, "I forgot the eggs."

"No eggs, no pancakes," Molly summarized.

"Not so fast, I can substitute for eggs," Anna retorted.

"Substitute?" Molly queried.

"Yup, I can use some of my jam, you wait and see," Anna proudly confirmed.

With that, Anna went to work mixing the pancake batter and presented quite the breakfast for Molly and her. Strawberry jam pancakes, warm maple syrup, sausage links, and piping hot coffee.

After breakfast, they had multiple cups of coffee as they sat on the porch, watching the sun hit the mountains as if it were trying to wake them up.

Glancing around the yard Molly spotted a small green building tucked amongst some evergreens. It had a white pipe sticking out of the roof.

"What's that?" she queried, as Anna stepped out with another cup of coffee.

"Ah, that's the outhouse, Molly," Anna proffered with a knowing smile.

"Out house?" Molly repeated— again with furrowed brows.

"You know," Anna shrugged her shoulders with Molly's obvious naivety, adding, "privy, latrine, backhouse, dunny."

Molly with her head somewhat bowed, eyes wide and raised just stared at her.

"Molly, it's an outside toilet," Anna enunciated, wondering if her friend had ever left the city before. "Especially for #2," she added, raising two of her fingers.

It was becoming quite obvious that Molly, even if she had left the city before, had never spent time in the woods.

"Guess I'm getting an education here," exclaimed Molly. "Sam's never going to believe this. Uh—oh, I was supposed to call him back yesterday and forgot," she sighed.

With that, Anna motioned for Molly to follow her back to the kitchen. There Anna instructed her to hold her cell phone near the wagon wheel hanging from the ceiling.

"That's about the only place in camp where you can get out,' Anna explained. She continued, "Cell service is pretty nil up here."

She stepped out so Molly would have some privacy while talking with her boyfriend.

Anna loved it at camp where it was always peaceful, that is, with the exception of her prankster husband. He was forever doing mischievous things. Another couple, Rose and Paul, had arrived to spend the weekend with them. Anna remembered the second night. It was pitch black outside. Rose being a little tipsy, excused herself from the group. They all watched while she carefully navigated the steps and groped her way through the darkness to the outhouse. They could hear her expletives, along with the snapping of limbs. Suddenly, a loud screech was followed by extremely colorful language and the slamming of the outhouse door. Minutes later, a not-so-tipsy Rose returned to confront the smirking prankster. Anna remembered how her husband had placed the owl on the eve of the outhouse. Its eyes would glow and it would hoot when anyone walked near. Anna couldn't help but chuckle as she relived the sight of his body doubled over with laughter—as she watched Molly open the door now.

"What's so funny?" Molly asked.

"Just remembering some of the pranks that have taken place here." Anna responded, shaking her head. "I've got to head for the outhouse," Anna announced.

"Number one or two?" Molly asked teasingly.

Anna flipped her what Molly took for the two sign—although she was not sure about that.

Anna proceeded to the outhouse thinking how Molly was coming around. She seemed much more relaxed then when she first arrived. And now, Anna recalled, Molly, finding her clothes a bit inappropriate for camp life, had reached out to her for more campy attire. She was thinking of all she was going to show Molly today—the Appalachian Trail, the Loop Road, Holly Brook, maybe they would see a moose. All this was going through Anna's mind when she sat down in the outhouse.

"Ahhhhhh, she screeched as water squirted up beneath her. "I'll get him for this," she hissed through clenched teeth. Continuing, she threatened, "He won't forget this."

Finishing her duty, Anna returned to find Molly standing on the porch.

"What happened, Anna?" Molly inquired, wringing her hands.

"Oh, he's going to pay for this one," Anna spurted, smiling

menacingly. "He rigged up the toilet seat turning it into a bidet—you know, a bum washer," she snapped.

"I know what a bidet is," Molly giggled, breaking into howl of laughter at Anna's expense.

Banishing the tension, Anna seeing a complete change in Molly since she had first arrived, smiled knowingly and erupted into roaring laughter herself.

"Come on Anna," Molly managed to say between guffaws of laughter. "Gimme some bug spray—let's check this place out," Molly chuckled"

After nearly taking a bath in bug spray, Molly donned a bug net and joined Anna for a walk around town . . . that is, around Hangtown!

Epilogue

The prankster created a tonic that brought visitors in a circle of relaxation, laughter, and, yes, survival. Share this experience with others. In this instance, forget the old adage 'What happens in camp, stays in camp.' Do not be so uptight with everyday life that you cannot enjoy the prankster, whose only intention is to make you and others chill and join in laughter. Take home some happiness and jolly times. Do not forget to laugh and relax, remember—Camp and Pranks.

Anna's Camp Larder

A Larder, which is a historical name for a place where perishable items were stored, changed purposes as refrigerators were introduced. In this case, Anna's larder was a tight-lid tote that kept the pesky mice at bay.

In her mouse proof Tote(s):
Coffee
Tea
All Purpose flour
Baking Powder
Baking Soda

Sugar/Honey
Dry Milk/Cremora
Olive and Canola Oil
Syrup
Salt & Pepper
Bouillon Cubes (Beef and Chicken)
Pasta (macaroni is the most versatile)
Garlic Powder or Salt
Onion Powder or Salt
Peanut Butter
Jam/Jelly
Hot Chocolate
Tequila
Triple Sec
Vodka
Whiskey
Anna's Camp Sangria
1 cup Anna's canned blueberry juice
2 cups Anna's canned Apple juice
¼ cup Honey*
1 cup orange liqueur**
1 lemon sliced***
1 cup strawberries sliced***

In a large pitcher combine the liquids and honey and stir well making sure the honey* is dissolved. Add the fruit and stir to combine the flavors. Refrigerate and let sit at least an hour. Anna likes to let hers sit overnight.

Just before serving Anna adds roughly 2 cups of sparkling water from her SodaStream. Sometimes she waits adding a squirt or two into each glass, then adds ice cubes and serves it!

*If she is out of honey, she makes a simple syrup: mix 1 cup water with 1 cup sugar.

**Triple Sec is a good substitute
*** Any fruit of choice can be used.

Anna's Pancakes:
1 Cup flour (whatever you have stored)
1 Tablespoon white sugar (brown sugar or Splenda works too!)
1 Teaspoon baking powder
½ Teaspoon baking soda
½ Teaspoon salt
2 Tablespoons jam (Anna used her strawberry rhubarb jam in place of the egg)*
2 Tablespoons butter
1 Cup milk

Mix dry ingredients together (this can be kept in a plastic container for later use). Add the wet ingredients and mix—do not overmix. Let batter sit for 5 minutes to thicken. Heat a greased skillet to medium high or less. Ladle batter into it. Cook the pancake until bubbly and flip. Repeat and enjoy!

*One can also use ½ ripe banana or ¼ cup applesauce or 3 tablespoons of peanut butter in place of 1 egg.

Chapter 25

WALKING HANGTOWN ROAD

THE ROAD, ONCE a lifeline for farmers and loggers, became a local dumping area for the camp owners around Pleasant Pond and the Pleasant Pond settlement during what locals call the paper company years. Now, it is mainly a camp road and a snowmobile trail in the winter months. A few camp and home owners along the road claim bragging rights to the road which is used by many walking, riding, sightseeing, hunting, bicycling, visiting or simply getting lost. Rights, because they, or at least some of them, have worked hard to keep the road passable, although many travelers think the "paper company" has done all the work! No town plowing, grading, or clearing of fallen trees on the rocky and pot-holed gravel road is done. Storm clean ups are usually done by the year-round residents, two at Hangtown , and two at the south end near Pleasant Pond.

The road runs north and south. I begin walking on the south end of the Hangtown Road heading north. On my left I pass Bateman's property with the red farmhouse and Charles Paddocks property to my right. Continuing on my left is Ken McAllister's vacant land where he is logging. Next is Charlie and Sue Hathaway's, then Paulette Thibodeau and Nathan Northrup's, then Jeff McAllister's, and Val McAllister's. Many owning a small piece across the road as well. As I move along, on the right William and Zara Saxton are building on their lot. I find myself stumbling downhill over an unforgiving ledge, sloshing through mud and a bit of wetlands with frogs peeping. And with more woods, the smell of the forest and, oh yes, the residue of ancient bottles and rusty cans from years gone by. Some are recently turned over, as if someone searched for a remembrance or a piece of history.

A small brook on my right reminds me of where the old schoolhouse had been. Situated between here and Holly Brook was the school, known as the Washington School, where Lila Rowe and Florence Sizeland once taught. All is gone now, but one can imagine the children's voices at recess, and one or two boys swinging buckets as they traipse down to the nearby brook to fetch water for the teacher or master. When the school was closed for good in 1917 there were four children in the school. Probably, Ethel Young's children- Walter, Ivy, Fred, and Flora.

Moving on to Holly Brook, I step lightly onto an old drooping bridge worn by years of traffic and aged by heavy use of logging trucks. I wonder how long this bridge over Holly Brook has been here and what was here before its construction. Did the residents in the early 1900s have a bridge or did they ford the rocky brook on horseback? Sometimes, perhaps, using wagons with iron rimmed wheels, like the circular iron I see washing and hung up on a small peninsula of earth and rocks below to my right. [This bridge was rebuilt in 2019 through the efforts of Hangtown camp owners, the local snowmobile club and Bayroot LLC, which donated some of the materials.]

I imagine hearing the clip clop of horse's hooves, perhaps those of Lawrence Hill's mare. Hill's farmhouse was just ahead, atop the rise on the right. I pass a carved wooden sign with an arrow pointing east onto the Appalachian Trail. Just to my left is where the slate was discovered.

As I crest Holly Brook Hill, I pause, stepping right, off the road and walking deeper into the woods. I step lightly over tumbled-down trees, to gaze at Hill's foundation and try to imagine what the Hill's farmhouse looked like. It is a beautifully built rock foundation outlining what must have been quite a large farmhouse, and still showing Marian's rosebushes now fighting for space in the overgrown field. This area now belongs to the Appalachian Trail System. The Trail, when crossing the road from the west to east, passes very close to that old foundation.

Back on the road again, on both sides of the road, the land is owned by Bayroot LLC, with Wagner managing it. On my left is a clearing, which was a logging yard, and a logging road is directly across from it. This is the Crossover Road which was built in 1997-98. It is still in use today as it crosses from the Hangtown Road to intersect with the Boise Road.

Hangtown, once home to sprawling farms with rolling fields of hay, buckwheat, oats, potatoes, is now littered with overgrown spindly trees left over from the tree harvesting for pulp and lumber. The farms were replaced by a few seasonal camps and a couple recent homesteaders tilling the rocky soil.

If I turn east on the Crossover Road, I would come to where evidence of Melvin's farm and well was. Just past this is a driveway that serves two camps. Alexander's camp is immediately on the left, and the Glidden's camp is straight ahead.

Back on the Hangtown Road, I walk north to pass two camps on my right. The first is DeRoche's camp, and Fuller's is next. Going further, on my left, is our homestead. A four-season camp, now our home! Owning the land across the road as well, I have a narrow trail that leads to my flower garden and abundantly producing vegetable garden. This land was once Andy Coone's homestead. He spent years homesteading here until he passed away. I pause and take a deep breath, remembering that morning when I found Andy, forever asleep in his favorite rocking chair. Memories of one of the most interesting individuals I have ever met quickly started tumbling back to me. Yes, a most interesting person—

Chapter 26

HANGTOWN'S HOMESTEADER ANDY

"HANGTOWN ANDY" HE was called by locals, "Homesteader" by fellow hikers, "Nurse Andy" by fellow workers, and "Brother" by his only living sibling.

Andy explored many options before choosing Maine and finding his niche at Hangtown. He was born in Raleigh, NC in 1951, the family later moved to Belvedere, SC where he graduated from High School in 1970. Between High School and college, Andy was employed by Camp Hope during the summers and worked with challenged students.

In 1974, he graduated from Clemson University with a degree in Microbiology. He went on to get his Master's Degree in Virology at Oregon State University in 1976.

Andy was an avid long distance hiker. By 1978 he had twice hiked the 2,200-mile Appalachian Trail from Georgia to Maine and accomplished this seven times in his lifetime. Later he hiked the 2,653-mile Pacific Crest Trail from the Mexican Border to the Canadian Border

---

[This trail travels through California, Oregon,
and Washington-and ranges in elevation
from 110 feet to 13,153 feet.]

Then there was his bicycle trip from Asheville, NC to Guatemala, heading back because of their civil war. He followed that with a bicycle trip to Mexico, where he stayed with a family for a month and learned their language before his return trip. Another trip took him bicycling around England. There were many other trips and hikes in the following years.

Andy was hired by Canaan Land Camps (Cape Hope), a girl's summer camp. In 1978, when it closed for the winter, Andy stayed on in one of their cabins. Wood was his only heat and he burned kerosene in his lamps for lighting. He had to hike nearly four miles for supplies.

Hiking different trails in the spring and summers, Andy easily made friends and was known by his trail name, Homesteader. Fellow hikers identified themselves with trail names such as Red Man, Tumbleweed, Mountain Goat, Slim Jims, Mac and The Silver Streak Steam-rolling Karen, Walkabout Bob and more.

Andy was one of many who left registers at the different shelters, requesting they get mailed to him when full. He left one at Jerome Brook, after finding one left by another hiker, and he wrote in it:

September 4, 1982: Andy Coone, Ga>Me (Georgia to Maine)

At last a register I can send back. I've wanted to send one to its owner the whole trip, and leave this one.

Last night was another moderate night hike night. We only walked a mile or so but it was through a wet and boggy area. I could tell it was wet because I could hear boots going squishy, squishy and someone would holler "Cow Pie".

Red Man just confessed he is ordering raw eggs at the carrying place tomorrow. I will have to leave the table.

Unfortunately the other register contained a good picture of Dave from Maine overdosing on caffeine and having the jitters, snorty comments on the sleeping conditions here, ratings of the outhouse, humor by Chiphead, and comments on a certain duo's hiking style. This one too will improve with age.

Patience everyone.

Many wrote in Andy's registers, some with great humor.

"9-9-82 Enjoyed sleeping on Little Bigelow last nite. Beauty always in a sunset & sunrise. Don't mind the dew on sleeping bag sights are worth it. Took a COLD QUICK DIP-swim in Flagstaff Lake. Onward today. Andy, what are you going to do with all these registers if and when you get them back? Glad you're leaving them. Great Buzz line!

Well thru-hikers how does it feel to be getting close to 'K'? Best wishes always.

St. Pete Steve Ga>Me"

Another for fun:
"6-12-83

I personally am getting a little irritated with the bug population of this state. MATC – how about getting some crews out and swatting a few of the nasty beasts, or maybe several hundred or maybe a couple thousand or a million or so of them??

PLEASE HELP – I'M GOING INSANE IN MAINE.

Nancy Me>No Bugs" (Maine to No Bugs!)"

On the trail again in 1988 Andy left a register at Hogback Ridge LT. The opening entry was written by him and certainly set the mood for more contributors.

"4-8-88 Andy Coone Ga>Sherman

I am now in the artic. All is white, all white. I am eating seal blubber. The wind is howling like wolves. Syd (sorry Syd, but you are not around so I will use your name mercilessly) has been eaten by a polar bear. I am all alone. I will go insane with the winter. In the spring I will marry an Eskimo woman. We will have all chubby, pink skinned children and name them after animals we have known. We will call them Swift Antelope and Mickey Mouse. I am writing like Thomas Wolf but using shorter sentences. Angels hover above the lean-to. Traversing the artic makes for a long day. Hopefully the snow will melt!"

These hikers became part of Andy's family and many he faithfully kept in contact with—some daily. In his own words found from an article in a 1978 issue of the Asheville Citizen – Times he wrote, "I really wasn't expecting the close family feeling the trail creates among hikers."

Observations of his that have stuck in my mind are, and I quote:

"Every hiker is every other hiker's neighbor . . . every hiker cares for every other hiker. And it is all natural, unforced . . . there is no barrier between hikers and no barriers to becoming a hiker, provided you have two legs . . . hikers have two things in common, a love of the woods and a positive attitude."

Another observation stuck with me even more: he writes:

"One thing that hikers and people of the towns along the trail have learned is that many good people are found inside the oddest exteriors."

As one townsman told Andy, "I've had some of the dirtiest people you could find sitting at my table but that's only dirt. You can wash that off. Hikers are the nicest people anywhere. It's just that sometimes they aren't the nicest looking."

Returning to college once again, Andy earned his LPN license from Haywood Community College. He continued taking classes to enable him to administer medicine and further his skills.

Before deciding to settle in Maine, Andy spent two years in Massachusetts. There he lived year-round in a tent equipped with a wooden floor and a wood-burning stove.

Moving to Maine 1990, where he trained to become a Maine Guide for white-water rafting. He also became a hiking guide and worked as a nurse. When he told us that he was once hired to cook breakfasts at the NLC—some place he never fully explained—we were shocked.

In response he blurted, "I can cook that stuff I just don't eat it."

Andy was a Vegan.

September 30, 1990, Andy purchased land on the Dyer's Road, Moxie and built a small home. He traveled a long graveled road to get to work.

Living so far from work, coupled with the difficult commute through winter snows and spring mud, convinced him to buy a more suitable place to live. It had to be remote and private. He bought land and a camp in Hangtown, The Forks Plantation. It was a large camp twenty-eight by thirty-two with one closed in loft. The camp had been built by Larry Fuller Sr. in 1996.

With plans to retire, Andy realized he needed a more economical and manageable dwelling. He decided to sell his old place with 3 acres of land and build a new home on the remainder. Being a very hard worker, Andy had the attitude that he could accomplish anything with hard labor and determination.

He built his Hangtown homestead, which eventually included a tiny house, sauna, outside shower stall, outhouse, screen house, sheds for storage that at one time housed pet hens. All built by hand. His hands!

Everything was done without equipment, only hand tools. He moved sand and gravel using partially filled five-gallon buckets from his old homestead, across a wooded, swampy trail, to the new location. His new gray water system was carved out by rugged muscles. Andy was five foot two-no fat, all muscle!

Andy chose to build high up on his property, near a big spring. He had no driveway—just a woods trail originating from Hangtown Road and reaching higher altitude with each step. I will never forget the first walk I took up that trail. The trail was crooked and a little rough, with exposed tree roots underfoot. Sometimes, I would have to stop and pick out the next turn, as it was very narrow and meandered through dense woods. Andy only cut trees when absolutely necessary, using only an ax or handsaw-no noisy smelly chainsaw for Andy!

I picked my way through shadowed woods, scattering squirrels to pine limbs, where they sat and scolded me for the invasion. My face, tangled in thin spidery webs crossing the trail, made me fear spiders crawling all over me. Suddenly, in front of me was a closed door. Yes, a door, with a window, in the middle of the woods, braced by two cedar poles and barriers on both sides, so you must pass through the door! There was no bell to ring, no sign to keep out—just the trail and more woods ahead. Shall I knock? I did!

Image 10. Andy's Door. Photo courtesy of Dottie Coon.

Passing through the door and with a few more steps brought me to an A-frame structure, roughly built but ready for company, with Adirondack chairs positioned in the small clearing. Resuming my hike, I emerged from the shady forest into full sunshine finding a magical garden with blooming flowers, bird feeders, and wind chimes. There

Andy was—dressed in an old shirt bearing frayed tails and ragged shorts with pockets held together with duct tape—making his way from his large vegetable garden to his hobbit-looking home.

Image 11. Andy's home. Photo by the author.

His large garden, which was almost on his A-frame's doorstep, provided an abundance of vegetables—enough that he shared with friends. He always left a few for the hikers on top of the wooden box outside the Caratunk Post Office. Beside his garden, he had mounded soil for a root cellar because digging a hole was not possible due to ledge being so close to the surface. In it he stored root vegetables such as potatoes, parsnips and squash which he often shared with us in the early spring.

Andy was frugal. He hated wasting anything that was useful or might become useful. Jackets and boots sported more duct tape than the opened roll did. His donned gloves either showed fingers or more duct tape or both! Oh, he had new clothes but these were kept for the seldom, special occasions, packed away in heavy black totes duct taped and stored out of doors.

Image 12. Andy's Garden. Photo by the author.

Many thought Andy was more or less the Hangtown Hermit. He readily took offense to this. One day, as we were talking before he took his crooked trail home, he burst out rather fiery: "I am not a hermit. Why would I be a nurse if I did not like being around people?"—this more of a statement than a question!

Andy liked solitude for time to think, and time to write, and time to plan projects. He relished the challenges that nature gave him and enjoyed proving himself with that positive attitude so treasured by him. Once when he was ill, I climbed his home trail to check on him, saying that I did not mean to intrude on his privacy. To my surprise, he responded that he didn't mind and enjoyed the company.

His home, was definitely a one-person abode, yet at one time he had two large dogs that shared the limited space. He built a small A-frame that only had sleeping quarters for overnight guests. A nearby spring was his source of water, which he carried in jugs. He had no refrigerator, so he placed a cooler in the spring, which collected and dispersed clean and cold spring water over the perishables. Being a vegan, he needed very little refrigeration for his foods. He raised his vegetables and canned them on an outside woodstove. He used kerosene for his lights and his Amish cook stove, which supplied his kitchen needs. On cool and colder nights, his heat from a woodstove supplied by wood from small trees that he chopped down and split by hand. A single solar panel and 12-volt battery powered his radio which provided talk-shows, a DVD player for Netflix, and a charger for his phone. He had to walk down his trail to Hangtown Road and near his truck to get cell phone service. Groceries, garden supplies, dog food and all other supplies had to be lugged uphill on the winding trail to his home. He hacked out other trails to and from his home. Some of them looped around his homestead, some accessed the Loop and Crossover Roads, and others meandered through scenic, peaceful woods.

Andy was a nurse. Winter mornings, he left for work around 4:30 am, strapping on his snowshoes and sometimes ice grippers to descend his steep trail. When he reached Hangtown Road, which becomes the snowmobile trail in the winter, he removed his snowshoes and hiked two miles south to his truck parked at Pleasant Pond. On his return trip, he loaded his backpack with necessities and hiked the two miles back to his trail. Once again he donned the snowshoes and maneuvered the crooked path to his home. He often dragged behind him a child's plastic or a tag-a-long sled, hauling heavy items such as 40-pound bags of dog food or 5 gallons of kerosene on the packed snow. Teasing him, I once suggested he put his now-only dog, Gandhi, to work and make him tow the sled. Gandhi looked like a big dog, with long and sometimes matted black hair—when shaved, he more closely resembled a skinny poodle. He was a big baby once he got to know you, but on their morning hikes, if a vehicle passed by, Gandhi would appear vicious. Andy would struggle to hold him, sometimes ending up in a snow bank. Andy usually managed to win the battle!

When Andy retired from nursing, he and Gandhi started training for a hike on Vermont's Long Trail to Canada. For years, they hiked daily for at least three miles and sometimes six, near their home. Finally, they increased their daily miles in preparation for the Long Trail hike. As they neared ten miles a day, Gandhi wore his own doggy-backpack to carry his food and treats, getting used to the weight. It was fun to watch them and their progress. The miles gradually increased from ten to fifteen to seventeen. Both man and dog seemed excited about their upcoming and possibly difficult journey. I always met them on their return exercise sharing conversation and progress with Andy—a pat and a milk bone for Gandhi.

*Image 13. Andy and Gandhi ready for
their hike. Photo by the author.*

Andy's house was very tightly built. He had used can after can of spray foam to fill cracks, especially between the siding and roof. He burned kerosene for lights and his unvented cookstove, producing toxic fumes in his tightly built home. Those same kerosene fumes and residue may have ultimately taken his life.

After not feeling well for days and undergoing various tests, he was diagnosed with prolymphocytic leukemia. A stay in the hospital, home, and medication was not adequate. Before further treatment could be started, Lon Andrew Coone—Hangtown's Homesteader Andy— died at his home in Hangtown twenty-one days after first falling ill. I sigh with the memory of finding Andy, forever asleep in his rocking chair . . . a peaceful end for one who enjoyed a peaceful life. He died as quietly as he lived and alone except for his faithful dog, Gandhi. Andy passed away on September 3, 2020. Gandhi was adopted by Hangtown neighbors and was nicknamed Hangtown Gandhi.

The gardens are still kept. Perhaps not as Andy would, but the best the new owner can do. The birds find plenty of food on their own and the chimes still sound in the breezes.

Image 14. New Owner's Garden. Photo by the author.

Chapter 27

RESUMING MY WALK

Again I sigh with those memories, and back on the Hangtown road I resume my walk to the Farrington camps #1 and #2, both on the right, which are the last camps I pass in Hangtown.

Further on at the apple orchard, I spook partridge high up in the apple trees, searching for the once-abundant apples. The apple trees have little chance for growth as the wind-wrecked evergreens have toppled into their over grown and tangled limbs. The arm-like limbs weighed down the trunks so heavily that their roots were torn from the ancient ground. The orchard is now an apple tree graveyard.

Winding through the downed trees, I come to the cellar hole where the Lovejoy's, and the Powell's house once stood. It peeks up through the wild gangly raspberry bushes, as if it is almost hinting at the past. A patch of pie plant, once supplying fruit for Lizzie's pies, is pushing up under the canopy of spruce and fir at the forest's edge.

Where are all the farms now? Where are those hardworking families with households up at dawn and not resting until the sun no longer gives them the light? And the kitchens filled with the warm yellow glow of kerosene lights in the evenings while the family awaited their men to return from the fields or winter logging? I imagine the smell of kerosene and wood smoke mingling with the aroma of the evening meal—perhaps caribou or venison roast with steaming vegetables from the root cellar, and plates of strawberry-rhubarb pie with fresh cream from the family cow. Why do I not hear the sweet voices of children when they tossed grain to their chicks? Where is the next homesteading generation?

These homesteaders are gone now from Hangtown. They moved to find work in paper mills, shoe companies, stores, and the like, a new life with a constant paycheck and jobs that only required an eight-hour day. Medical aid could be found within minutes—not hours traveled on a rough and sometimes impassable snowy woods road—perhaps as the patient lingered near death. These once-homesteaders now earning a steady paycheck, could afford luxuries they never had before. Now they could give their children things they never had. No more dawn to dusk in the fields and woods. No miles to walk to schools and stores. They hoped to put hardships to rest.

The north end of Hangtown is owned by Bayroot LLC and managed by Wagner Forest. Being of no use to them, the Hangtown road that once reached all the way to the Kennebec River at The Forks and Route 201 ends here at the north end. Perhaps one day it will be reopened for the tree harvesting. All the farms are gone. The once horse and oxen-cleared fields are now overgrown with trees and the rampant growth of moosewood. The apple orchards, barely clinging to life, are choked off from the sun by uncontrolled trees and their own unpruned massive limbs.

Hangtown Road was once a serviceable road until the forest started tumbling down. The north end is impassable now, not even for walking. What was once a beautiful jaunt filled with the smell of spring blossoms, birds calling, squirrels' warning, the chatter of chipmunks, and the beating of the partridge wings has become inaccessible. That part of the road is blocked now by uprooted and fallen trees. The history encased in tree growth, seemingly forever.

As I come to the end of the over-grown Hangtown road there is a feeling of nostalgia. I look back at the bush-filled cellar holes, the bits and pieces of rusted farm equipment, the flat land beneath the forest canopy where the homesteaders had cleared the land for hay and potatoes, and those piles of rocks as they did. I see where skidders in later years furrowed paths to haul out harvested trees. I lean on my walking stick, which I have used to clear the spider webs before they hit my face—as if they are trying to web my eyes to prevent me from seeing or feeling—or perhaps to slow me down, as if urging me to listen and feel the energy these settlers gave to this land—to Hangtown!

THE END

Appendix

The Census Years

The names are listed as they appear in the pages of the census; including spelling.

M=males F=females

1820 T1 R4 North of Caratunk

Tracia Howe

1830 T1 R4 East of the Kennebec

Heads of household; with number of members in each household (including head)

John Bumpus	4	(3m, 1f)
Lasky Kallier	4	(3m, 1f)
Daniel Williams	11	(7m, 4f)
William Homes*	4	(1m, 3f) *probably spelled Holmes
Warren Bumpus	5	(4m, 1f)
Jacob Williams	6	(2m, 4f)
William Steward	7	(5m, 2f)

1840 T1 4th Range: 5

Thomas McGuire	4	(2m, 2f)

| Thomas Berry | 1 | (1m) |
| David S. Young | 5 | (1m, 4f) |

1850 T1R4 East of the Kennebec:

Jno Holway	5	(3m, 2f)
Seth Baker	9	(3m, 6f)
Francis Williams	7	(5m, 2f)
Robert Love	5	(2m, 3f)
Richard Spaulding	5	(4m, 1f)
Samuel Moore	9	(6m, 3f)
Jno Kimball Jr.	6	(2m, 4f)
Andrew Kennedy	4	(1m, 3f)
Joseph Spaulding	21	(11m, 10f)
Samuel Suckling	3	(1m, 2f)
Edward Webster	11	(6m, 5f)
Jonah Sterling	7	(4m, 3f)
Lavina Chase	6	(4m, 2f)

1860 T1R4 East of the Kennebec

Robert Love	10	(6m, 4f)
John Ham	7	(4m, 3f)
Joseph McKneeley	8	(6m, 2f)
Cyrus Young	7	(4m, 3f)
James Meservy	7	(2m, 5f)
Joseph Runnels	3	(1m, 2f)
Charles Durgin	7	(3m, 4f)

Johnathan Spaulding	7	(5m, 2f)
Hiram Moore	3	(2m, 1f)
Daniel Williams	9	(6m, 3f)
John Dorothy	5	(4m, 1f)
Mary A. Powell	3	(2m, 1f)
Henry Durgin	5	(4m, 1f)
Patrick McDay	3	(2m, 1f)
Charles Williams	6	(3m, 3f)
James M Young	11	(5m, 6f)
Richard Morris	9	(7m, 2f)
Orren Bryant	3	(2m, 1f)
Samuel Moore Jr.	1	(1m)
Mary Shephard	6	(3m, 3f)
Samuel Moore Sr.	2	(2m,)
Robard Forsaith	6	(5m, 1f)
Laskey Jackson	8	(3m, 5f)
John Steward	4	(3m, 1f)
Thomas McKue	2	(1m, 1f)
John Holway	13	(6m, 7f)
William Steward	1	(1m,)
Moses W Burnham	8	(3m, 5f)

[This does not include Bowtown]

1870 T1 R4 East of the Kennebec

| Smith Spaulding | 8 | (6m, 2f) |
| Ameziah Murry | 15 | (10m, 5) |

Seth Adams	7	(3m, 5f)
Jery B Durgin	1	(1m,)
John Holway	7	(4m, 3f)
Oliver Adams	7	(2m, 5f)
Charles W Williams	3	(2m, 1f)
Cyrus P Young	8	(5m, 3f)
Elijah Hall	2	(1m, 1f)
James M Young	4	(2m, 2f)
Irving Young	3	(2m, 1f)
William Lockwood	5	(2m, 3f)
Thomas Morris	9	(6m, 3f)
James Burwood	6	(3m, 3f)
Samuel Moore	1	(1m,)
John L Ham	7	(4m, 3f)
William Adams	6	(3m, 3f)
Robert Forsyth	9	(5m, 4f)
John B Adams	6	(4m, 2f)
Frederick Bulett	2	(1m, 1f)
John Murphey	6	(4m, 2f)
John Stewart	8	(3m, 5f)
John Garden	4	(1m, 3f)
Charles A Williams	2	(1m, 1f)
Joseph Pooler	5	(2m, 3f)
Albert Spaulding	8	(4m, 4f)
Michael Martin	10	(7m, 3f)

1880 T1R4 East of the Kennebec

Albert Spaulding	5	(2m, 3f)
John Hall	3	(1m, 2f)
Lawrence Hill	4	(2m, 2f)
David Devoll	7	(3m, 4f)
Henry Lovejoy	8	(4m, 4f)
Justus Adams	5	(3m, 2f)
Jeremiah Hill	10	(6m, 4f)
Michael Martin	4	(3m, 1f)
Patrick Martin	4	(2m, 2f)
Winfield Powell	9	(4m, 5f)
Charles Williams	5	(2m, 3f)
James W Steward	2	(1m, 1f)
James Powell	7	(4m, 3f)
Edwin Morris	6	(4m, 2f)
Robert Forsyth	7	(4m, 3f)
Chester Bates	5	(1m, 4f)
John Ham	3	(1m, 2f)
Sarah Moore	8	(4m, 4f)
William Adams	7	(2m, 4f)
William Lockwood	6	(3m, 3f)
William Morris	6	(1m, 5f)
Charles Williams	5	(4m, 1f)
Johnathan Bean	11	(7m, 4f)
Cyrus young	6	(2m, 4f)

Sylvester Bumpus	7	(3m, 4f)
J. S. Spaulding	8	(5m, 3f)
James M Young	3	(2m, 1f)
Jeremiah B Durgin	1	(1m,)
Edward Crotto	5	(3m, 2f)
Seth Adams	5	(2m, 3f)
John Holway	8	(4m, 4f)
Joseph Clark	10	(5m, 5f)
Frank Heald	1	(1m,)

1890 No U.S. Census exists for this decade.

1900 T1 R4 East of the Kennebec

Anthony Comber	5	(3m, 2f)
James Powell	8	(4m, 4f)
William Sizeland	4	(2m, 2f)
James Melvin	5	(3m, 2f)
Lawrence Hill	3	(2m, 1f)
Charles A Williams	5	(2m, 3f)
James Stewart	5	(3m, 2f)
Winfield S Powell	7	(4m, 3f)
Millard French	5	(3m 2f)
William Forsythe	3	(2m, 1f)
George Markham	6	(4m, 2f)
James Merrill	12	(10m, 2f)
Charles York	6	(4m, 2f)

Charles Ball	3	(2m, 1f)
Michael Martin	2	(1m, 1f)
John Comber	8	(4m, 4f)
Larry (Comber?)	3	(2m, 1f)
James Hunnewell	10	(7m, 3f)
Cyrus Young	5	(2m, 3f)
Ethel Young	4	(3m, 1f)
George Durgin	3	(2m, 1f)
Michael Kennedy	4	(2m, 2f)
Edwin Morris	8	(6m, 2f)
Andrew Farley	3	(1m, 2f)
Manley Bean	6	(2m, 3f)
Morris Bean	5	(2m, 3f)
Alexander Boulard	4	(3m, 1f)
George Wilson	5	(1m, 4f)
Hiram Pierce	3	(2m, 1f)
Charles Pierce	2	(1m, 1f)
William Young	5	(2m, 3f)

1910 T1R4 East of the Kennebec

Allen Worster	7	(2m, 5f)
Herbert Greely	2	(1m, 1f)
Edwin Caswell	1	(1m,)
George Gould	2	(1m, 1f)
Bertie Laxson	7	(1m, 6f)
Harry King	1	(1m,)

Seward Tucker	3	(2m, 1f)
James O'Brien	4	(2m, 2f)
Charles York	3	(2m, 1f)
Frank Fitzsimmons	5	(4m, 1f)
William Young	6	(4m, 2f)
Lovina Bragg	3	(2m, 1f)
Davis Pierce	8	(5m, 3f)
Alexander Harris	5	(2m, 3f)
Hiram Pierce	2	(1m, 1f)
James McGilvery	2	(2m,)
Ethel Young	6	(3m, 4f)
James Powell	6	(3m, 3f)
William Sizeland	4	(2m, 2f)
Anthony Comber	4	(3m, 1f)
Forrest Williams	5	(4m, 1f)
James Stewart	7	(4m, 3f)
Winfield Powell	9	(6m,3f)
John Comber	5	(3m, 2f)
George Merrill	6	(2m, 4f)
Andrew Farley	6	(2m, 4f)
George Durgin	3	(1m, 2f)
Edwin Morris	10	(9m, 1f)
Rod McPherson	1	(1m,)
Robert Harvie	7	(3m, 4f)
Dumont Bean	7	(5m, 2f)

Jonathan H Bean	3	(2m, 1f)
Charles Hackett	2	(1m, 1f)
Walter Durgin	13	(9m, 4f)
George Wilson	5	(1m, 4f)
James Kinsley	2	(1m, 1f)

1920 T1 R4 East of the Kennebec

Archibald Murry	3	(1m, 2f)
John Bradley	2	(1m, 1f)
Arlon Low	5	(2m, 3f)
Fred Owen	1	(1m,)
John Sneedburg	4	(2m, 2f)
Axel Sneedburg	9	(7m, 2f)
Silas Perkins	4	(2m, 2f)
Andrew Lawrence	9	(6m, 3f)
George Merrill	10	(5m, 5f)
Wilson Holway	3	(2m, 1f)
Fred Harris	5	(2m, 3f)
Alexander Harris	8	(5m, 3f)
Fred Marshall	5	(2m, 3f)
William Adams	9	(4m, 5f)
Herbert Durgin	3	(1m, 2f)
Walter Durgin	4	(2m, 2f)
Charles Hackett	2	(1m, 1f)
Alfred Durgin	2	(1m, 1f)

Lyford Beane	5	(3m, 2f)
Jonathan Bean	4	(3m, 1f)
Edwin O'Neil	6	(4m, 2f)
Henritta B Durgin	1	(0m, 1f)
David Pooler	7	(2m, 5f)
Allen O'Neil	8	(4m, 4f)
Terrence Martin	2	(1m, 1f)
William Hunnewell	4	(1m, 3f)
Nathaniel Arn	7	(4m, 3f)
Mark Morris	3	(1m, 2f)
James Stewart	3	(2m, 1f)
Forrest Williams	3	(2m, 1f)
William Comber	2	(1m, 1f)
James Powell	3	(3m, 0f)
John Dubois	1	(1m, 0f)
Ethelred Young	5	(3m, 2f)
William Sizeland	1	(1m, 0f)

The population for The Forks is still climbing until midcentury.

Population of The Forks over the years-

1900	157
1910	169
1920	153
1930	144
1940	123

1950   45 Perhaps the war, WWII, caused the decline.

1960   53

1970   45

1980   72

1990   30

2000   35

2010   37

2020   48

The population starts to decline in the 40s. The decline is more than likely do to logging days gone by; farms being sold perhaps because of war; the men away with their wives and children running the farm. Some brave men never made it home. There was plenty of work available in factories and industries. There was the increase of summer residents, and whitewater rafting which had started in The Forks in 1976 increased summer population only.

Sources Consulted

Books

Adams, Azel. Creative Survival: A Narrative History of Azel Adams, the Forks Maine. Old Bess Publishing Company, 1992.

Allen, Ardelle "Ida." Ida: A Happy Life in the Maine Backwoods. Thorndike Press, 1979.

Dale, T. Nelson, Edwin C. Eckel, W. F. Hillebrand, and A. T. Coons. Slate Deposits and Slate Industry of the United States. U.S. Geological Survey Bulletin No. 275. Government Printing Office, Washington, D.C., 1906. Accessed online via U.S. Geological Survey Publications Warehouse.

Hall, Jon F. The Upper Kennebec Valley, Arcadia Publishing, 1999.

Kalloch, Norman R., Jr. A Long Way to Walk: One Family's Tragic Journey Through the Maine Wilderness. Maine Author's Publishing, 2018.

Macdougall, Walter. The Old Somerset Railroad: A Lifeline for Northern Mainers. Down East Books, 2000.

McAllister, Donna. The Sesquicentennial History of Caratunk, Maine. Caratunk History Committee, 1990.

Sterling-Gondek, Marilyn. The Forks of the Kennebec: Sources for an Early History. Old Canada Road Historical Society, 2017.

Tatelbaum, Linda. Carrying Water as a Way of Life; A Homesteader's History. About Time Press, 1997.

Archives & Databases

Ancestry.com..Genealogical Records Database (including user-submitted phtographs). Accessed on line, 2019–2025.

Chronicling America. Historic American Newspapers. Library of Congress.

Fold3. U.S. Military Records Database. Accessed for information on James Powell Sr.

Maine Department of Education. Data Warehouse.

Somerset County Registry of Deeds (Skowhegan, Maine). Online Land Records Database. Accessed various dates.

Spaulding, Abby M. Diary. Old Canada Road Historical Society, Bingham, Maine.

Town of The Forks Plantation, Maine. Records, Reports and Maps. Accessed in person, 2019–2025.

U.S. Census Bureau. Census Records and Data. Washington, D.C.

U.S. Census Bureau. Non-Population Census Schedules (Agriculture), 1850–1880.

U.S. Geological Survey. Historical Topographic Map Collection. Reston, Virginia: U.S. Department of the Interior. Accessed 2023.

Wikipedia. "Balm of Gilead." Wikipedia. The Free Encyclopedia.

Wikipedia. "Bayroot LLC." Wikipedia. The Free Encyclopedia.

Wikipedia. "Placerville, California." Wikipedia, The Free Encyclopedia.

Wikipedia. Umbagog. Accessed n.d.

Newspapers

"Obituary." Bangor Daily News (Bangor, Maine), April 18, 1934.

Asheville Citizen-Times (Asheville, North Carolina), 1978.

Portland Daily Press (Portland, Maine), 1885.

The Independent-Reporter (Skowhegan, Maine), 1909–1955.

The Somerset Reporter (Skowhegan, Maine), 1868–1909.

The Somerset Reporter (Skowhegan, Maine), 1955–1987.

Maps

Google Earth. Satellite Imagery and Map Resource. Google LLC. Accessed 2019–2025.

Library of Congress. Digital Collections and Maps. Accessed 2019–2025.

Maine State Archives. Maps and Land Office Records. Augusta, Maine.

Maine State Archives. Forest Colby Map, Township 1 Range 4, BKP EKR, The Forks Plantation. Land Office Maps and Plans, 1903.

Somerset County Survey Maps and Town Plots, 18th–19th Century. Maine State Archives.

U.S. Coast and Geodetic Survey. Nautical and Topographical Maps. Washington, D.C.

Images

Image 1. Bingham's Purchase, 1792. Courtesy of the Maine State Archives.

Image 2. Flagstaff and Forks Plantation map, 1860. Courtesy of the Library of Congress.

Image 3. Early settlers in Pleasant Pond area, 1860. Courtesy of the Library of Congress.

Image 4. Southern section of The Forks Plantation, 1883. Courtesy of the Library of Congress.

Image 5. American Realty Company. Survey Map of Township 1 Range 4, Maine. 1903. Maine State Archives.

Image 6. Burnham's Lot. G.N. Colby's 1860 map. Courtesy of the Library of Congress.

Image 7. Location of the school, Topographical Map, 1905. Courtesy of the U.S. Coast and Geodetic Survey / NOAA.

Image 8a. Balm of Gilead tree and cabin. Photo by the author.

Image 8b. Balm of Gilead and tractor. Photo by the author.

Image 9a. William E. Sizeland's Farm. Photo courtesy of William H. Sizeland.

Image 9b. William E. Sizeland. Photo courtesy by William H. Sizeland,

Image 10. Andy's Door. Photo courtesy by Dottie Coone

Image 11. Andy's home. Photo by the author.

Image 12. Andy's garden. Photo by the author.

Image 13. Andy and Gandhi ready for hike. Photo by the author.

Image 14. New owner's garden. Photo by the author.

Oral Histories

Oral Histories and Stories from residents of The Forks Plantation, The West Forks, Caratunk, and Bingham, Maine. Accessed in person, 2019–2025.

Image Index